Praise for VIOLENCE AMONG US

We know Brenda and Paula. They know the world of abuse. But they also know the Lord. These two courageous, vulnerable, godly women are calling the church to speak into the world of abuse with the reality of Christ. And this book helps equip the church to speak well. The church has many callings. This is one that is too often neglected. Read this book, *Violence among Us: Ministry to Families in Crisis*, and let it stir you to action.

—Dr. Larry and Rachel Crabb, Newway Ministries
Authors, speakers, and seminar leaders

I have known Brenda Branson and Paula Silva for many years. They have a track record that is unexcelled when it comes to understanding the issue of domestic abuse. I always have found their work to be impeccable and their insights to be intelligent. *Violence among Us: Ministry to Families in Crisis* is no exception. I highly recommend it to pastors, women's ministry directors, Sunday school teachers, and lay persons who care about the families around them who, often behind closed doors, are imploding with abuse. Someday we all will give an account for what we have done in this life, so may we be educated and responsible in our response to the victims of abuse and their abusers.

—Jan Silvious, Author, *Foolproofing Your Life*

Based on years of experience, both personal and professional, Brenda Branson and Paula Silva have written an honest, uncompromisingly truthful book on domestic violence that reaches a complex audience (abused, abusers, church, pastors, counselors, neighbors and friends of the abused, and Christians everywhere) in the most educational, comprehensible, and practical of ways. The value of this document cannot be overemphasized; besides being enlightening and convicting, it is inspiring and motivating. It is also a great resource in its basic education, its psychological insight, and its appendixes rich with titles, websites, and treatment programs.

—Dr. Rosalie de Rosset, Professor of Communications and Literature,
Moody Bible Institute, Chicago, Illinois

The pain of domestic violence cries in silent sobs in our homes, schools and colleges, social groups, and even churches and Bible studies. *Violence among Us* tunes us into the cry of the broken and hurting and provides the action plan we need to respond effectively. This book is a great resource for anyone who is involved with a group of people—teachers, pastors, small-group leaders, and even parents. It is a must-read for every authority figure who sets policy and the procedures for responding to crises.

—Eileen Warren, CADC III, CCSI
MW2A Counseling, Inc.

How do you help a frantic wife who calls your home late one night to say her husband, an officer in your church, has threatened her and she fears for her life? *Violence among Us: Ministry to Families in Crisis* will prepare you for a quick response that protects this distraught member as well as assisting you in avoiding the common mistake of doubting that the alleged perpetrator could do such a thing. Are there warning signs of domestic violence in your church? This book will highlight these signs and help bring families together.

—Rev. Ronald L. Siegenthaler, Executive Minister
Coral Ridge Presbyterian Church, Ft. Lauderdale, Florida

Here is a book that exposes the well hidden secret of abuse within the home—yes, even the Christian home! As a pastor I long ago concluded that those of us in leadership must create an atmosphere where victims can safely tell their story and get the help they need. My prayer is that this book will be widely read and be used to give mothers and children the courage to go for help rather than suffer the long term consequences of abuse. And those who read this book will be ready to provide a helpful response when the need arises.

—Dr. Erwin W. Lutzer
Senior Pastor, The Moody Church, Chicago, Illinois

It would be easy to think that the increasing level of domestic violence in America, and unfortunately in the Christian church, is a problem too big to solve and that we might as well call it quits, give up and wave the white flag of surrender to this deplorable and tragic reality. However, in this book, Brenda and Paula reduce the problem down to bite-sized pieces so that even regular people like you and me will discover that, "Hey, I can do this. I can make a difference. I can help save someone." This is not a read-and-shelve kind of book; this is a read-and-do kind of book.

—Steve Dresselhaus, TEAM missionary and pastor,
La Paz de Cristo Church, La Paz, Mexico
Director, La Paz Women's Shelter

VIOLENCE AMONG US

Ministry to Families in Crisis

BRENDA BRANSON / PAULA J. SILVA

FOREWORD BY TIM CLINTON

JUDSON PRESS
PUBLISHERS SINCE 1824
VALLEY FORGE

Judson Press has made every effort to trace the ownership of all quotes. In the event
of a question arising from the use of a quote, we regret any error made and will be
pleased to make the necessary correction in future printings and editions of this book.

Bible quotations in this volume are from the following:
  The Holy Bible, King James Version (KJV).
  HOLY BIBLE: *New International Version* (NIV), copyright © 1973, 1978, 1984.
Used by permission of Zondervan Bible Publishers.
  The Holy Bible, New Living Translation (NLT), copyright © 1996. Used by per-
mission of Tyndale House Publishers, Inc., Wheaton, IL 60189. All rights reserved.
  The New King James Version (NKJV). Copyright © 1972, 1984 by Thomas Nel-
son Inc.
  The Holy Bible, English Standard Version (ESV), copyright © 2001 by Crossway
Bibles, a division of Good News Publishers. Used by permission. All rights reserved.

Library of Congress Cataloging-in-Publication Data

Branson, Brenda.
    Violence among us : ministry to families in crisis / Brenda Branson, Paula J.
Silva ; foreword by Tim Clinton. — 1st ed.
        p. cm.
    Includes bibliographical references.
    ISBN 978-0-8170-1515-2 (pbk. : alk. paper) 1. Church work with problem
families. 2. Family violence—Religious aspects—Christianity. 3. Family—Religious
aspects—Christianity. I. Silva, Paula J. II. Title.
    BV4438.5.B73 2007
    259'.1—dc22   2007002846

Printed on recycled paper in the U.S.A.

First Edition, 2007.

Trev, this book is dedicated to you. You're my hero! I'm proud of the man you've become and pray for you to become all God created you to be. You are truly a gift from God to me—the best son I could have ever asked for. I love you . . . more.

—Brenda Branson

In loving memory of my mom and dad, Harold and Rae Dean Hanson, who consistently loved and encouraged me and introduced me to Jesus Christ, the best gift I could ever receive. John, Amy, and Charity (and their wonderful spouses), this book is also dedicated to you. God has blessed me with wonderful children who are serving God and who have given me my precious grandchildren.

—Paula Silva

Contents

Foreword

As she sat down she was noticeably anxious. Her heart was pounding, her breathing was erratic, and she was visibly shaking. Thinking she needed a minute to gather herself, I asked her if she needed a drink. That's when she tearfully launched into a vivid description of what *he* did to her.

Two days prior her husband had "gone off."

"He grabbed me by the neck and choked me until I couldn't breathe anymore," she cried. "I passed out. Just look at me."

The bruises looked like two thumb prints and multiple fingers that had reached around to the back of her throat.

"Tim, I couldn't breathe."

She wasn't remembering the incident; she was reliving it in front of me. In the world of counseling, we call this trauma.

I couldn't help but think and feel my way through this moment. Part of my mind went to my own daughter—thinking what I would do if this happened to her. Then the Holy Spirit gently moved *my* spirit back to *God's* daughter seated across from me. My focus intensified.

No one deserves to be abused. No one deserves to be on the back hand of someone's anger. Such violence mars the soul. I believe God hates such atrocity and calls us to rescue, advocate for, and protect those who are violated. In my estimation, the church has been silent for too long on this subject, and it's time we make a course correction.

Violence among Us: Ministry to Families in Crisis shoves us in the right direction. Bold, brave, and clear in their resolve, Brenda and Paula offer hope, healing, and direction for those who hurt and those who help. You may or may not agree with everything they have written, but one thing is sure—it is the best work to date available. I have no doubt that God will use their words to help save many individuals and families.

Read and be blessed. I was.

Dr. Tim Clinton, LPC, LMFT, BCPCC
President, American Association of Christian Counselors
Author of *Turn Your Life Around: Breaking Free from Your
Past to a New and Better You*

Acknowledgments

Not to us, O Lord, but to you goes all the glory for your unfailing love and faithfulness.

—Psalm 115:1, NLT

I'm so very thankful to God, my Father, for his open arms of protection and provision each step along my journey; to Jesus, my Redeemer, for his unchanging, faithful love; and to the Spirit, my Life Coach, for his continual presence and instruction. God, you've restored my life, renewed my joy, and infused me with passion for living and loving others. My greatest treasure is your presence, and the desire of my heart is to know you more and reflect your love and beauty. I'm overwhelmed by your mercy in using the brokenness of my life for your service. All glory and honor is yours alone.

Special thanks to mentors, family, friends, and colleagues who have had an impact on my life in profound ways:

To **Larry and Rachael Crabb** for teaching me the value of brokenness, the love of community, and the joy of dancing with the Trinity.

To **John Townsend and Henry Cloud** for teaching me about boundaries and relationships the way God designed them to be.

To **Todd Agnew** for challenging me to dig deeper into the Word; for being an example in reflecting Jesus to others, especially those who are broken and hurting; for your amazing voice and music that stir my soul to deep worship; for teaching the Word in ways that spark new life in old stories; and for your passionate love for God. Also to **Brian, Jon, Cody,** and **Rob** for your ministry onstage with Agnew and in your personal lives. You have blessed and enriched my life and enhanced my worship. I love all of you guys!

To **Jan Silvious** for your practical wisdom from the Word.

To **Liz Curtis Higgs** for being such an example of grace and for having a wonderful sense of humor which is a healing medicine to wounded souls.

To **Sarah-Rebecca Bennett** for your creative artistry.

To **Mom and Dad** for your love and support.

To **so many others** left unnamed who have prayed faithfully, listened and affirmed, shared your stories, provided assistance, challenged my thinking, provided community, and walked along-side—you know who you are! I'm thankful to God for all of you.

—Brenda Branson

Let your unfailing love surround us, Lord, for our hope is in you alone.

—Psalm 33:22, NLT

I am so grateful to God for never abandoning me, for lifting me out of the pit, accepting me just as I am, and calling me to be a vessel for him. I stand in awe of my Lord that he would use my painful experiences and shattered dreams to make a difference in someone else. He has been so faithful to me showering me with endless love and blessings. What a privilege it is to be in an intimate relationship with God, Jesus Christ, and the Holy Spirit, knowing that a way will be made when there seems to be no way.

My heart is full of gratitude to all those who have walked this journey with me, giving me wisdom, guidance, and support:

To **Henry Cloud** and **John Townsend** for teaching me about boundaries, a lesson that became the turning point in my life.

To **Larry and Rachael Crabb** for revealing how my relationship with the Trinity can transform my life.

To **Jan Silvious** for helping me to learn how to deal with a fool biblically.

To **Liz Curtis Higgs** for helping me laugh in the midst of despair and teaching me God's view of women.

To my counselor, **Anna Marie Lafrentz,** who taught me to see myself through God's eyes.

To my brothers, **Rick** and **Jim** (and wives), for your love and support.

To my church, **Harvard Avenue Evangelical Free Church,** that embraced me and FOCUS Ministries, Inc.

To all my special friends, family, and those I have met along the way for challenging me to discover who I am in Christ.

—Paula Silva

Introduction

> The LORD looked and was displeased to find that there was no justice. He was amazed to see that no one intervened to help the oppressed. So he himself stepped in to save them with his mighty power and justice.
>
> —Isaiah 59:15-16, NLT

Since the founding of FOCUS Ministries, Inc.,[1] in 1995, we have been reaching out to women in crisis who are struggling in abusive and dysfunctional relationships. Most of them belong to churches like yours. Statistics show that one in every four women in each church community is being abused by her partner or has been abused at some time in the past. One in every four—*count them!* How many women does that make in your congregation?

Our purpose in writing this book is to encourage and equip you to minister effectively to families who are being ripped apart and destroyed by an insidious enemy who has sown the seeds of abuse and violence since the creation of humankind. We want to do more than dispel the common myth that the victim did something to provoke or deserve abuse. We also want to destroy the illusion that abuse is the result of stress, anger, loss of control, or addictions. Our goal is to help you see beneath the symptoms of abuse to the underlying spiritual issues.

The challenge for every pastor and counselor is to go beyond a casual awareness of the problem to the harsh reality of this epidemic, to move past apathy to conviction, and to turn empathy into compelling action. As spiritual leaders and Christ-followers, your mandate from God is to come alongside hurting people and join the battle for their hearts and souls.

Now is the time for the body of Christ to wake up, shake off its lethargy, and represent Jesus to its fellow travelers and to a world of lost, lonely people who need hope and healing. So roll up your sleeves, prepare yourselves for battle, set the standard, educate the troops, equip the saints, prepare a strategic offense, deploy those to administer physical and spiritual healing, designate safety zones, provide sustenance, commit to the long rebuilding process, boldly confront and renounce evil, proclaim liberty, defend the defenseless, and reflect Jesus to those who are hurting.

This is your wake-up call—a call to action: "Rescue those who are unjustly sentenced to death; don't stand back and let them die. Don't try to avoid responsibility by saying you didn't know about it. For God knows all hearts, and *he sees you*. He keeps watch over your soul, and *he knows you knew!* And he will judge all people according to what they have done" (Proverbs 24:11-12, NLT; italics added).

Note

1. FOCUS Ministries, Inc., PO Box 323, Hanson, KY, 42413 or PO Box 2014, Elmhurst, IL, 60126; website: http://focusministries1.org.

CHAPTER 1

Discovering Her Journey— Validating Her Pain

> Jesus was on his way to Jerusalem to die for the salvation of all mankind. Even though he was on the way to do *the* most important thing in the history of mankind, his ears still heard the cry of the broken and hurting, and he stopped what he was doing because someone needed him.
>
> —Todd Agnew, telling the story of blind Bartimaeus[1]

When you hear the cry of the broken and hurting, how do you respond? Are you compelled to turn compassion into action? Or perhaps you're too busy to get involved in messy situations where you may be asked to trade your comfort for other people's lives—people like Bethany and Bill.

When Bethany married her high school sweetheart, Bill, she trusted him completely, looking to him as the spiritual leader of their home. Bill was charming and likeable. As the son of a missionary pastor, he knew the Bible from cover to cover.

Although Bill and Bethany appeared to be a loving couple at church on Sundays, behind closed doors he was a batterer who controlled and assaulted Bethany with caustic words and closed fists. The man with whom she had chosen to spend the rest of her life threatened her with guns and knives. For thirteen years she endured verbal, psychological, spiritual, sexual, and physical abuse.

Bethany represents 31 percent of all married women who will experience physical violence in their marriage.[2] Keep in mind, these are just the reported cases of physical abuse that can be measured by statisticians and do not take into account unreported or nonphysical assaults.

By the time Bethany arrives in your office, she has become emotionally numb. She appears to be in suspended animation, convinced by her abuser that she is a total failure needing to be "fixed." Life seems meaningless and hopeless. Through years of verbal, emotional, physical, and sexual assaults, Bethany has experienced death—death of her dreams, death of her future, death of herself.

She does not reach out to others for fear of not being believed and to protect the reputation of her husband. She wonders if God really cares, and if the Lord does care, whether he really has the power to change things.

Bill has misused Scripture to justify his behavior. In the fallout from each abusive episode, he has convinced Bethany that God was angry at her and would punish her for ruining the marriage. She is a hostage in her own home, in her own skin—a nonperson paralyzed by fear and shame.

Your Response

As her pastoral counselor, how will you breathe life into Bethany's soul? Your counsel will either keep her in bondage or provide options that lead to spiritual and emotional freedom to become the woman God had in mind when she was created.

Listed below are three scenarios describing a possible response to Bethany's initial visit. Which one best describes how you would handle this difficult situation?

Response 1: Get Both Sides

Because you have known Bill for many years, you have trouble believing he is capable of doing the things Bethany has described. You will call Bill later today to get his side of the story. Thinking Bethany may be overly sensitive or suffering from an emotional breakdown, you feel it is in the best interests of the church to ask her to step down from her teaching position in children's church. Doing so will allow her to focus on her marriage, you explain. Then you ask Bethany to identify a time next week when she and Bill can meet with you together. Bethany seems hesitant to schedule another meeting, so before she leaves you pray together for God to give Bethany courage to do the right thing.

Response 2: Prioritize the Marriage – Starting with Her

As a pastoral counselor, you believe your primary goal is to help couples reconcile. After Bethany shares her story, you outline a course of action that begins with Bethany—encouraging her to work on her unforgiving attitude and offering tips on how to avoid pushing Bill's buttons. You recommend weekly counseling sessions with the couple and give Bethany a brochure about a weekend marriage retreat where the couple can reconnect. Before Bethany leaves, you pray with her for God to heal the marriage and give her strength to work harder on changing her own behavior.

Response 3: Secure Her Safety First

After Bethany shares her story, you assume she is telling the truth and ask strategic questions to determine her level of safety. You offer several options and wait for her response. If she is in imminent danger and willing to accept help, you take immediate action to provide shelter by placing her in a safe home, a hotel, or the local women's domestic violence shelter. You also contact a church or agency that will respond immediately to meet her needs. Offer her your support if she chooses to contact law enforcement or seek legal advice from an attorney.

Reflecting Jesus

Which scenario reflects Jesus as he stood and read: "The Spirit of the Lord is on me, because he has anointed me to preach good news to the poor. He has sent me to proclaim freedom for the prisoners and recovery of sight for the blind, to release the oppressed, to proclaim the year of the Lord's favor" (Luke 4:18-19, NIV).

Ponder that question until we examine all three scenarios in depth in chapter 9, "Counseling Dos and Don'ts." Regardless of the scenario you choose, the first step is to listen without judgment to the victim's story and then to validate her pain. Clearly communicate that God does not condone abuse, that the Lord wants us to be safe. Even if you wonder about the accuracy of her story (after all, Bill is this great guy who is well respected in the church), your most important responsibilities are focusing on what Bethany is telling you and acknowledging the anguish she is experiencing. In most cases, victims will share only the tip of the iceberg to check your reaction to see if revealing more is safe. A wise pastor or counselor will ask questions and remain alert for signs of abuse as her story unfolds—both in the details she offers and in her body language and word choice as she describes her situation.

Impact of Denial

Is domestic violence occurring in your church? As stated in the introduction, one in every four women in the American church has experienced family violence.[3] If you haven't done so already, do the math to determine the total for your church.

That some pastors are unaware of the scope of this problem is not surprising. Many women are ashamed to admit they are having problems at home. They hide behind plastic smiles and pretend everything is okay so their dysfunctional home life will not be exposed to other families who appear to be perfect.

Some churches teach that a godly woman should endure abuse as her cross to bear to win her husband. As a result, too many women choose the support of the church and the blessings of the pastor rather than safety.

In addition, some pastors completely deny the existence of this problem in their church. This denial insulates them and the congregation against the problem; therefore, they don't have to get involved. When an abuser denies the problem exists in his family, he continues his violent behavior without suffering any consequences. When the victim denies abuse to protect her husband and to keep the family intact, she continues to suffer and puts her children at risk.

How widespread is the problem?

- According to the U.S. Department of Justice National Crime Survey, a woman is beaten in her home every nine seconds.[4]
- Approximately three million women are physically abused by their husbands or boyfriends each year.[5]
- Nearly one-third of American women (31 percent) report being physically or sexually abused by a husband or boyfriend at some point in their lives.[6]
- In 2001 more than half a million American women were victims of nonfatal violence committed by an intimate partner.[7]
- In 2001 women accounted for 85 percent of the victims of intimate partner violence (588,490) and men accounted for approximately 15 percent of the victims (103,220).[8]
- Every day in the United States, more than three women are murdered by their husbands or boyfriends.[9]
- Fifty percent of all homeless women and children in America are fleeing domestic violence.[10] Yet the United States has three times more animal shelters than shelters for woman and children fleeing family violence.[11]

Health Issues

- The leading cause of injury to women between ages fifteen and forty-four is abuse by a partner. More women are treated in emergency rooms for battering injuries than for muggings, rapes, and traffic accidents combined.[12]
- Victims of domestic violence account for 22–35 percent of all women seeking emergency medical care. An estimated $150 million in medical expenses result from domestic violence injuries.[13]
- As many as 324,000 women each year experience violence from a partner during their pregnancy.[14]
- Homicide is the leading cause of death overall for pregnant women, followed by cancer, acute and chronic respiratory conditions, motor vehicle collisions, drug overdose, peripartum and postpartum heart disease, and suicide.[15]
- Battering during pregnancy is the leading cause of birth defects and infant mortality—more than birth defects caused by all

diseases combined for which people are routinely inoculated.[16]

- The health-related costs of rape, physical assault, stalking, and homicide committed by husbands or boyfriends exceed $5.8 billion each year. Of that amount, nearly $4.1 billion is for direct medical and mental health care services, and nearly $1.8 billion is for the indirect costs of lost productivity or wages.[17]

Although these statistics are startling, they represent only reported cases of physical abuse. Other types of abuse are rarely reported, and even women who report physical abuse suffer in silence. You may never meet these women in your office for counseling, but their voices need to be heard because their pain is real.

Silent Voices

Rhonda sings in the choir. As she smiles and sings wonderful songs of encouragement to the congregation, her own life is filled with fear and despair. She has endured years of verbal abuse and constant criticism that she isn't meeting her husband's needs. She has tried everything she knows to please him, but nothing ever does. When she talked to him about a separation, he threatened, "If you ever leave me, I'll kill you and then I'll kill myself." Rhonda knows he is serious. Guilt and terror buy her silence.

Amanda is a faithful church member who helps out in the youth group. Few people know that Amanda's husband has a violent temper that often erupts right before they leave for church on Sunday mornings. Once he was ticked off because she chose a short-sleeved shirt for him instead of a long-sleeved one. After slapping her face and threatening to deal with her later, he ordered her to wipe away her tears and straighten up. During the service, Amanda experiences fear and anxiety in anticipation of their return home. Will he still be angry? Will he hit her again or will she have to endure an afternoon of criticism, lectures, and verbal battering?

Ruth often asks for prayer for her family's financial needs. What people don't realize is that Ruth is covering up a serious breakdown in her marriage. Her husband shadows her wherever she goes to make sure she doesn't tell anyone about family business. If she is talking on the phone when her husband arrives home from work, she abruptly ends the call so he won't be angry. Ruth can't even go to the grocery store without her husband alongside. He monitors every purchase and criticizes her choices. Even though she works part time, she is expected to turn over her paycheck to him. She has no idea how much money they have and must ask him for spending money if she exceeds her monthly allowance. She feels like a prisoner in her own home but is too humiliated to tell anyone.

Carol is in her seventies. Although she attends church activities for seniors and enjoys socializing with other women in her Sunday school class, she does not feel free to share her past. They would be surprised to find out that Carol's ex-husband isolated her from her grown children and forbade her even to talk to them on the phone. He packed the handset of their phone in his briefcase when he left for work so she couldn't make or receive calls while he was away. Having suffered years of psychological abuse, Carol finally escaped after being held at gunpoint by her husband. Her wounds are deep and she is not comforted by Sunday morning smiles or evangelical sermons.

Stories like these are played out every day in respectable, upscale neighborhoods as well as in rundown, poor areas of towns and cities throughout the United States. This epidemic has spread to the people next door and the family sitting next to you in the pew at church. You may not immediately recognize the face of this evil. Abuse isn't only the physical violence inflicted by fists or weapons such as guns and knives. As women like Rhonda, Ruth, and Carol can testify, money, words, emotions, sex, and relationships can be wielded as weapons of psychological and emotional violence when a spouse seeks to control through any means available. You may not hear the cries of the victim until foundations begin to crumble and families are ripped apart. What will your response be?

You have three choices: One, you can insulate yourself, your church, and your family by pretending the problem isn't as bad as statistics indicate—certainly not in *your* congregation.

A second choice is to put the issue on the back burner until you are forced to deal with it; you are extremely busy and don't want to get entangled in messy issues that may lead to divorce. Keep incidents quiet and resist in-depth or long-term involvement for fear of legal or financial consequences.

Your third choice is to step up and get involved. Educate and equip your congregation by teaching about and preaching against family violence. Develop a ministry strategy for intervention and protection. Establish an emergency fund for meeting the victims' critical financial needs. Research and publicize a list of resources, including shelters, counselors, social services, and legal aid agencies.

As you minister to families in crisis, ask God to give you the compassion of Christ to move beyond good intentions to love in action. Then ask for courage to go the distance. For helping victims of domestic violence in La Paz, Mexico, missionary pastor Steve Dresselhaus has been threatened with guns, machetes, and other weapons. He wrote, "My church needs to know that serving Christ is an action lifestyle, not an academic one."[18]

Love in action is no less important than evangelism. Our plea to pastors and churches is to get as involved in saving lives as you are in saving souls. Our challenge to all who read this book is best expressed by quoting the words of Todd Agnew, a musician and modern-day prophet who has impacted many lives for the kingdom:

God has no backup plan to save the world. God has no backup plan to feed the hungry. The government is not part of his plan— it's the church. God has no backup plan to free the imprisoned, no backup plan to clothe the naked, no backup plan to house the poor. It's just us—we're the plan.[19]

If we are the plan, then we need to identify the enemy and understand his strategy for destroying precious lives. Chapter 2 explores the dynamics of family violence and offers a glimpse into the trauma and secrecy more common in church-going families than anyone ever imagined.

Notes

1. Todd Agnew, during live concert, Cornelia, GA, on May 19, 2006 (www.ToddAgnew.com). Ardent Records (www.ardentrecords.com), VanLiere-Wilcox Management (www.vanlierewilcox.com). See Mark 10:46-52 for the story of Bartimaeus.
2. Katherine Scott Collins, Cathy Schoen, Susan Joseph, et al., *Health Concerns Across a Woman's Lifespan: 1998 Survey of Women's Health*, The Commonwealth Fund, May 1999.
3. Patricia Tjaden and Nancy Thoennes, "Extent, Nature, and Consequences of Intimate Partner Violence," National Institute of Justice and the Centers of Disease Control and Prevention (July 2000). In our experience over the last decade and more, we have found these statistics to be as true in the Christian community as in larger society.
4. U.S. Bureau of Justice National Crime Survey and FBI statistics, Family Violence Prevention Fund, 1998.
5. Collins, et al.
6. Ibid.
7. Callie Marie Rennison, "Intimate Partner Violence, 1993–2001," *Bureau of Justice Statistics Crime Data Brief*, February 2003 (Washington, D.C.: U.S. Department of Justice, Office of Justice Programs).
8. Ibid.
9. Ibid.
10. Dawn Bradley Berry, *The Domestic Violence Sourcebook* (Lincolnwood, IL: Lowell House, 2000), 10.
11. Catherine Clark Kroeger and Nancy Nason-Clark, *No Place for Abuse: Biblical and Practical Resources to Counteract Domestic Violence* (Downers Grove, IL: InterVarsity Press, 2001), 70.
12. Berry, 8.
13. "Interpersonal Violence against Women Throughout the Life Span," Fact Sheet, American College of Obstetrics and Gynecologists. http://www.acog.org/departments/dept_notice.cfm?recno=17& bulletin=186 (accessed July 11, 2007).
14. J. A. Gazmararian, et al. "Violence and Reproductive Health: Current Knowledge and Future Research Directions," *Maternal and Child Health Journal* 4, no. 2 (2000): 79–84.
15. Angela Nannini, Judith Weiss, Rebecca Goldstein, and Sally Fogerty, "Pregnancy-Associated Mortality at the End of the Twentieth Century: Massachusetts, 1990–1999," *Journal of the American*

Medical Women's Association 57, no. 23 (Summer 2002): 140.

16. Berry, 9.

17. National Center for Injury Prevention and Control, *Costs of Intimate Partner Violence Against Women in the United States* (Atlanta: Centers for Disease Control and Prevention, 2003), 2.

18. Steve Dresselhaus, personal e-mail to Brenda Branson, 2006. Used by permission.

19. Todd Agnew, during live concert, Union, SC, on May 20, 2006 (www.ToddAgnew.com). Ardent Records (www.ardentrecords.com), VanLiere-Wilcox Management (www.vanlierewilcox.com).

CHAPTER 2

Understanding the Dynamics
of Family Violence

Violence not only adversely affects each member
of the family, but potentially destroys future
generations as the vicious cycle perpetuates.

—FOCUS Newsletter, October 1999

D omestic violence is a learned behavior that can be unlearned.
However, the roots of abuse must be clearly identified and
replaced by renewed values in the heart and mind of the abuser so
that he treasures and respects his wife more than his need for
power and control.

Bob and Jane live next door to Tim and Sue in a middle-class
neighborhood in the suburbs. Both couples attend the same
church and their children ride the bus together to school. From all
outward appearances, both families appear to be loving parents
who provide a healthy home environment for their children. They
are well respected in their neighborhood, at work, and at church.

Yet behind the walls of one of these homes a well-kept secret
hides—a secret that may not be obvious to their neighbors,
friends, or family, and perhaps not even known to their pastor.
Each member of the family guards the secret, sometimes for
decades, as if telling anyone would detonate a hidden explosive
that would destroy them all.

What is the secret? *Things are not as they seem.* While family
members smile and act like a so-called normal family in public, in

private they tiptoe around, as if on eggshells, to keep from triggering an explosion. They live on an emotional roller coaster, never knowing whether to expect fun and games or rage and destruction—never knowing whether they are going to awaken a gentle giant or an angry ogre.

Good times are celebrated for all to see and bad times are swept under the carpet as if nothing happened. Members of this family feel like a person living in two dimensions—one in the light where they pretend everything is okay and another in the dark where they live in terror of saying or doing the wrong thing.

Bob and Jane's home represents freedom and growth. Family members are free to make choices and express their opinions respectfully, and mistakes are handled with grace and forgiveness. When Bob and Jane need help with difficult issues in their marriage, they respond well to couple's counseling or a marriage retreat where both work together as equals.

Tim and Sue's home represents oppression and repression. Tim makes all the decisions and defies anyone to cross him. Sue knows better than to express an opinion that does not agree with Tim's. When someone makes a mistake or fails to live up to Tim's standards, he rages and metes out punishment, usually blaming Sue for anything that goes wrong. Fear of retaliation and fear of abandonment keep Sue and the kids from telling their secret to anyone else. When (and if) Tim and Sue seek help with difficult issues in their marriage, couple's counseling creates an uneven playing field. Tim feels justified in pointing to Sue as the scapegoat and manages to manipulate the pastor or counselor by diverting attention from the real issues. Instead of helping this couple grow, marriage counseling places an additional burden on Sue to work harder to apply techniques that work only in a mutual relationship.

Because secrecy and pretense hide abusive families in plain sight, pastoral counselors must be alert to signs that identify domestic violence and must learn to ask the right questions. A good place to begin is to understand the definition of domestic violence.

Emerge, a Boston counseling program for abusive men, defines *domestic violence* as "forcing one's partner to do something that they don't want to do or preventing them from doing what they want to do. This definition includes physical violence and threats of violence, but it also includes psychological, mental, sexual, and economic abuse."[1] The National Center for Victims of Crime (NCVC) defines the term as the "willful intimidation, assault, battery, sexual assault, or other abusive behavior perpetrated by one family member, household member, or intimate partner against another."[2] In our own ministry, FOCUS, we define domestic violence as a "repeated pattern of behavior used to instill fear and gain power and control over another person through the use of intimidation, emotional abuse, verbal abuse, sexual abuse, or physical assault."[3]

Legally and morally, a single act of physical or sexual violence must be deemed domestic violence, but what is the difference between an occasional verbal disagreement and emotional or verbal abuse? The key distinction we see is the continuous pattern of behavior that can be tracked over a period of time. Often described as a cycle of abuse, the pattern begins with building tension (walking on eggshells), is followed by a violent outburst of verbal and/or physical assault, and often reverts to a period of calm (referred to as "the honeymoon period" or "good times"). As one partner dominates and controls the other through fear, humiliation, or assault, the cycle starts all over again.

The cycle of abuse cannot be traced in every abusive relationship because some abusers, described as cobralike in their behavior, strike at random without any buildup of tension. They have little if any remorse following their attack. Although their victims perceive them as frightening, they often appear extremely charming to everyone else.

When people define domestic violence, physical assault is frequently the first thing that comes to mind. However, just as insidious as physical assault are other types of abuse, which are often dismissed by pastors and counselors as nonthreatening. These include intimidation, emotional abuse, financial control, verbal abuse, spiritual abuse, and sexual assault. The next chapter provides a glimpse into the lives of several women who describe oppression and domination by husbands who don't "get their hands dirty" by inflicting physical assault. Perhaps their stories will help you feel their pain from wounds you cannot see.

Of course, many abusers use a combination of tactics to maintain power and control. If verbal and emotional abuse don't keep a person "in line," an abuser may begin strict financial control. When intimidation and threats are no longer effective, the abuser may isolate the victim from family and friends and resort to physical or sexual assault to instill fear and obedience.

A pastoral counselor who observes one partner dominating and controlling the other through fear, humiliation, or assault should assume domestic violence is occurring in the home. If personal observation is not revealing, listen for words from the victim that indicate she must ask permission before making any decisions on her own. Be sensitive to disparaging remarks she makes about herself that may be a reflection of verbal abuse in the home. Don't dismiss her fears and anxiety as irrational just because she is not being assaulted physically.

What follows are tactics that can be defined as domestic violence within the definition of a repeated pattern of behavior used to instill fear and gain power and control over another person.

Emotional Abuse

- Intimidating, humiliating, and manipulating
- Withholding emotional support
- Using the silent treatment
- Exerting financial control
- Undermining a partner's authority as a parent or in relationships with other people
- Destroying pets or personal property
- Deliberately causing confusion ("crazy making")
- Badgering
- Deceiving or lying
- Depriving sleep
- Driving recklessly
- Isolating from friends and family
- Threatening to harm the victim or her children, friends, or family

Verbal Abuse

- Name calling
- Shaming and insulting
- Ridiculing and demeaning
- Using words or tone of voice to destroy self-worth
- Accusing and blaming
- Using profanity or sarcasm to demean, insult, or ridicule

Sexual Assault

- Forcing sexual intercourse (rape)
- Demonstrating sexually degrading attitudes
- Compelling involvement in frightening or unpleasant sexual acts
- Imposing reproductive decisions

Physical Assault

- Slapping, hitting, and punching
- Pinching and poking
- Beating with an object or pummeling repeatedly with fists
- Kicking
- Choking
- Shoving, pushing, and grabbing
- Pinning down and restraining
- Twisting limbs and pulling hair
- Burning, binding, and chaining
- Throwing things across the room
- Locking out of the house or car
- Blocking exits
- Attacking with an object
- Using deadly weapons

Spiritual Abuse

- Distorting Scripture by taking it out of context (see chapter 5 for common examples)
- Misusing concepts of "headship" and submission to exert power and control

- Invalidating a partner's belief in God
- Condemning the partner to hell when she fails to measure up to the abuser's expectations or demands

Many additional behaviors could be added to each of these lists, but this provides a glimpse into the complicated dynamics of domestic violence. Enduring just one of these tactics on a regular basis would be devastating, but many victims are exposed to most or all of these behaviors during the course of their marriage or significant relationship.

It may be impossible to conceive that the person you have known for years, served with on boards and committees, ministered alongside in church and community, is capable of such behavior. It is natural to look for excuses or explanations to dismiss the ugly charge or suspicion. However, before you allow yourself to ask the question "What did she do to provoke him?" remember the cycle of abuse and the variety of tactics used by a clever perpetrator to instill fear and gain power and control. Keep your focus on the abusive behavior and hold the abuser accountable for his actions instead of blaming the victim.

Even if you get a glimpse of the problem through personal observation or by talking with the victim, many layers of secrecy must be uncovered before you see the whole picture. Don't minimize the seriousness of the situation just because the victim seems to be functioning well emotionally and physically. She may not even realize she is in an abusive situation, being unable to admit to herself that she could be a victim or that her husband could be an abuser. Although she realizes the relationship is difficult, she may not realize the extent of existing destructive patterns until her husband's behavior is identified as abusive, sinful, illegal, and harmful to the entire family structure.

The next chapter will examine more closely various types of spousal abuse and their impact on the victim. *All* abuse hurts!

Notes

1. http://www.emergedv.com/dvfaq.html (accessed July 11, 2007). Emerge: Counseling and Education to Stop Domestic Violence, 2380 Massachusetts Avenue, Suite 101, Cambridge, MA 02410, 617-547-9879, www.emergedv.com.
2. National Center for Victims of Crime, GET HELP Series. http://www.ncvc.org/ncvc/main.aspx?dbName=DocumentViewer &DocumentID=32347 (accessed July 11, 2007).
3. "Train the Trainer Seminar," FOCUS Support Group Leaders' Training Manual (Elmhurst, IL: FOCUS Ministries, Inc., 2004), 28.

CHAPTER 3

All Abuse Hurts!

Emotional battering . . . runs the gamut from a steady grinding down of a woman to emotional trauma. While her bones are never broken, her flesh never bruised, her blood never spilled, she is wounded nonetheless.

—Mary Susan Miller, *No Visible Wounds*[1]

Carolyn endured fifteen years of emotional and verbal abuse. She was so used to being ridiculed and blamed for everything that went wrong, she thought being treated that way was normal. She tried to make peace by taking the blame for her husband's outbursts, but no matter what she did—being more submissive, attempting to reason with him, praying more, trying harder to improve her appearance and actions—the abuse did not stop. She was the receptacle for her husband's rage and contempt. One day he showed his contempt in front of a witness as he cleared his throat and spat on Carolyn's face while she cowered from his vicious verbal attack.

Because Carolyn's husband kept his hands clean by not assaulting her physically, she could not call the police for help. They would not arrest a man for hurling verbal missiles that pierce as deep as any knife wound but leave invisible scars.

Emotional and verbal abuse are often minimized by pastors, counselors, friends, and family because the wounds are not as visible as a broken arm or split lip. Yet if you ask women who have experienced both physical and emotional abuse, most will say emotional and verbal abuse is worse. Most physical wounds heal eventually, but the wounds of the soul and spirit can take decades, and sometimes a lifetime, to heal.

Emotional Abuse

These wounds of the soul and spirit include intimidation, humiliation, and manipulation; financial control; destroying pets and property; crazy making, deprivation of sleep, deceiving, lying; driving recklessly, intimidation and threats; and isolation and using other people.

Intimidation, Humiliation, and Manipulation

When a person's dignity is stripped away, controlling and manipulating her becomes easier. The abuser stomps on the victim verbally and emotionally until she feels like a nonperson. He thus elevates himself in his own eyes to a powerful conqueror who has won control of his castle. He convinces her she is ugly, incompetent, or unworthy of his love and attention by comparing her to other women. She works harder and harder to adjust her appearance or behavior to suit him, but he constantly raises the bar, making it impossible to meet his expectations.

Carolyn described herself this way: "How can God love a person like me? I feel so worthless. My husband tells me I am trash and treats me that way emotionally and physically. Why would anyone love me? I feel so dirty sometimes, like people can see right through this ugly person. I don't think anyone understands what a person who is supposed to love you can do to you."

Financial Control

Instead of working as a team to develop a budget, an abuser takes control. He expects his wife to turn over her paychecks to him, and in return he gives her a small allowance. She must provide receipts to justify how her allotment is spent and is totally at his mercy when she needs additional funds. Instead of being an equal partner, she is forced into a parent-child position where she must ask his permission just to go out for lunch with friends. He may keep her completely unaware of their financial situation so she won't know he is hiding assets or listing only his name on bank accounts and real estate or automobile titles. In an opposite scenario, a passive-aggressive abuser will manipulate and undermine his wife by placing all financial responsibility on her shoulders while constantly criticizing her decisions and making her the scapegoat for their financial difficulties. Economic control can also mean keeping her from getting a job or providing her with everything she needs as long as she asks for the money.

Mary's husband would not allow her to work outside the home. He kept her a virtual prisoner by withholding all money from her. He drove her to the grocery store and gave her cash to buy groceries for the family while he waited inside the car for her to return with the receipt and change. Because he set limits on how many diapers she could buy each week, she was faced with the dilemma of either allowing the baby to wear soiled diapers or running out before the next grocery-shopping trip. He decided whether she could buy clothes for the older children or let them go without. Even though the family had medical insurance, she needed his permission to take the children to the doctor. These severe restrictions imposed by her husband left Mary feeling helpless as a parent and put her children at great risk.

Destroying Pets and Property

The goal of an abuser is to maintain control over the actions, thoughts, and emotions of another person. One way to do that is by destroying things that are precious to her—treasured artwork and homework papers of a child, family heirlooms, a beloved pet.

Susan had one small closet in which to store her personal belongings and one shelf at the top of a stairwell for her books. Because he wanted the space for himself, Susan's husband gave her notice that she must remove her belongings from the closet before he got home from work or he would throw everything away that evening. She was forced to store her things in a dilapidated garage full of spiders and roaches. When her husband arrived home that evening, he flexed his "power muscle" by taking her books to the damp basement where they eventually were ruined from mildew and mold. In spite of Susan's compliance with her husband's demands, he threw away a box containing drawings and cards made by their children that Susan had treasured and protected for several years. Although he inflicted no physical wounds, Susan's husband assaulted her in the most vulnerable place possible—her heart.

"Crazy Making," Sleep Deprivation, Deception, and Lies

These tactics create confusion in the mind of the victim, which gives the abuser a false sense of power and insulates him from being confronted by the truth about himself. If he can keep the victim off balance and convince her and others that she is crazy or out of touch with reality, the focus shifts from his behavior to her sanity.

Joan's husband delighted in giving her orders to clean out the basement or other chores around the house. When she reported the jobs were done, he denied asking her to do them and criticized her for not doing certain other things. He fed her tidbits of false information, making her look foolish to others when she repeated what she thought was true. Joan's husband took sick pleasure in forcing her to stay awake late at night as he ranted and raved. At times he kicked her out of the bedroom, forcing her to sleep on the couch. Several times throughout the night, he yanked the blankets off her and pushed her off the bed onto the floor. No wonder Joan suffered from chronic fatigue and anxiety attacks. She explained her situation this way: "I lost fifteen pounds, was getting no sleep and little to eat, and started experiencing severe chest pains. I was numb emotionally. I just wanted it to end; however it was going to end was fine with me."

Driving Recklessly, Intimidation, and Threats

These tactics create fear and anxiety. Two common methods abusive men use to instill fear without resorting to physical violence are ranting and raving and quietly intimidating their spouse or partner. Ranting and raving includes using threatening words, tone of voice (screaming, low guttural raging that increases in intensity), slamming doors, and throwing objects. Quietly intimidating another person includes stalking, threatening to harm someone or himself, displaying weapons, "the look" that instills fear, and driving recklessly.

Barbara's husband slept with a machete under the bed and often woke her up in the middle of the night saying he needed his gun to blow her away. One day on her way to church, he followed her in his car and tried to run her off the road. He often appeared out of nowhere in the parking garage at her workplace to check up on her and would leave notes on the windshield of her car to let her know he was watching.

Isolation and Using Other People

An abuser knows that isolating his wife cuts off her source of support from others and makes her more dependent on him. He may accomplish this by disabling her car, monitoring her phone calls, reading her mail and e-mail, criticizing her family and friends, preventing her from attending social activities, or moving together to a remote location without public transportation. He may influence other people to turn against her by telling them she is having a mental breakdown or by telling them things she said about them that she didn't actually say. He may also undermine her authority as a parent by manipulating the children's trust in her ability to care for them.

Lisa's husband undermined her sense of self-worth by telling her negative things about herself that he said he had heard from the women at church, which they didn't really say. He tapped the phone lines to listen to her conversations during the day and even packed the telephone handset in his briefcase at times to prevent her from making or receiving calls. When Lisa went to her pastor for help, she wondered why he was so distant. She learned later that prior to her visit, her husband had planted in the pastor's mind seeds of doubt about her mental stability and had accused her of the very things he had actually done to her. Instead of offering help, the pastor asked Lisa to step down from her duties at church until the issues at home were resolved.

Verbal Abuse

Verbal abuse tears down a person's esteem and rips apart the heart and soul. It is a vicious tactic used by an abuser to shred a person's dignity piece by piece. When a group of women was asked how being verbally disrespected felt, individual responses included:

> "I was ashamed."
>
> "I lost myself to the extent that I hardly knew who I was anymore."
>
> "I felt as if I was the most worthless being on earth, as if I deserved it."
>
> "I felt like my spirit and soul were being butchered and ripped apart."
>
> "I had worked for years and supported myself, traveled extensively, and was very independent. I had high self-esteem and was confident. I knew who I was, what my limitations were, and was content with my life and myself. Even with that foundation, when the man you love more than anyone on earth repeatedly calls you names and says you are nothing but dirt, after a while it wears on you."

Name Calling, Accusing, Ridiculing, and Demeaning

By calling her names, the abuser slaps a label on his partner that defines her. At times he may yell profanities or rant and rage, accusing her of an affair or some evil behavior. This frightens, confuses, shames, and humiliates her. He may make her feel stupid by criticizing her appearance, cooking, parenting skills, or housekeeping. When she shares her ideas and dreams, he uses sarcasm to demean and belittle her intelligence and insight. By denying her experience or discounting her feelings, the abuser destroys the victim's self-perception. He may refuse to communicate or he controls what can be discussed by diverting the subject from his behavior to flaws he finds in her.

Sexual Abuse

When God's intention for sexual intercourse and intimacy is misused, through both sexual actions and attitudes, the violation affects far more than the physical body. The wounds go deep into the heart and soul.

Sexually Degrading Attitudes

An abuser may be addicted to pornography and have unhealthy attitudes toward sex that make his partner feel degraded and used. Many women report feeling like a prostitute instead of a marriage partner who is cherished.

Toni's husband had a sexual addiction and often told her if she would perform to his expectations, his sexual needs would be met and he would not have to look to sources such as pornography, adulterous affairs, pedophilia, or masturbation for self-gratification.

Forcing Sexual Acts or Reproductive Decisions

Many abused women have sex with their husbands out of fear. He may feel in control by demanding sex whenever he wants it, but she feels violated. Abusive sexual behaviors may range from actual rape to demanding the victim's participation in acts that are unpleasant, demeaning, or painful. Refusing to allow the victim a voice in reproductive decisions is another form of sexual abuse. One woman's husband would not allow her to use birth control. She was kept under his control at home with nine children.

Physical Assault

The American College of Emergency Physicians observes, "Although data is difficult to collect and interpret, studies have indicated that women seeking care in an emergency department for any reason are often victims of domestic violence."[2] Many people limit their definition of physical abuse to a serious injury that requires medical attention. However, physical abuse also includes any act intended to instill fear by the abuser using his physical strength to control his partner's behavior. This includes holding her down or blocking her exit. Many abusers deny assaulting their wives because they "just slapped her across the face." Some pastors and counselors also minimize any physical assault that doesn't require medical attention.

One pastor was called to the emergency room to attend to a

church member whose abusive husband hit her on the head so hard that she lost consciousness. Although the couple had a long history of physical abuse, the pastor believed the woman made up the story to get attention because the MRI did not show any sign of injury. Bruises or lumps on the head often do not show up until the day after an assault, making it difficult for doctors or police to make an accurate assessment of injury.

Here are two accounts from women who were assaulted by so-called Christian husbands:

"He was stronger in one of his hands than I was in my whole body. When he drank and got that animal look in his eyes, he got even stronger. I was terrified. When he came after me, I would make myself limp and crumble to the floor. Once I tried to fight back. He began twisting my wrist. I tried to bite him to make him let go, but he punched me in the mouth with the back of my own hand."

"He tried to strangle me once and, gasping, I told him, 'Go ahead. I'll be in heaven and you'll go to jail.' He squeezed harder and told me he could kill me and not spend a day in jail. Then I had to get the fine bones in my throat and neck adjusted, because he damaged them so [much that] it was hard for me to swallow or talk."

Spiritual Abuse

Many abusive men misuse Scripture to justify their bullying behavior in the home. The most common beliefs that are exploited are male headship and female submission. For example, a husband may emphasize Ephesians 5:22-24, overlooking the fuller context of verses 21-33; similarly, 1 Peter 3:1-6 is "preached" while neglecting verses 7-12. Some men justify their desire to control their partners by claiming their position as head of the home, paraphrasing and manipulating Ephesians 5:23-24 and 1 Timothy 4-5 to their own advantage. However, instead of imitating Christ's love and servant leadership, these men become tyrannical rulers instead of spiritual leaders. A sad fact is that more than a few churches encourage husbands to rule with an iron fist and to do whatever is necessary to keep their wives and children in line.

Husbands feel entitled to punish their wives if they deem them to be disobedient or insubordinate.

Submission, a principle taught in the Scriptures, describes the relationship of the Trinity as a model for all creation. However, in some belief systems the beauty of submission has been distorted into martial law applying only to women and children, giving abusive men an excuse to exert power and control over their households. A woman in this situation feels imprisoned, silenced, and oppressed as she is expected to submit to every whim of her abusive husband or face punishment, the wrath of God (according to her husband's distorted beliefs). Regrettably there are too many churches that endorse (or fail to contradict) such misappropriation of the biblical text.

Nowhere in the Scriptures is a man given the right to control, punish, or abuse his wife. Abusive men dishonor Paul's exhortation for husbands to imitate Christ as servant leaders in the home by emulating Jesus' love, respect, self-sacrifice, compassion, submission, and forgiveness. These are attributes of the Trinitarian union that should be reflected in the family and the church.

Steve Dresselhaus, missionary pastor in La Paz, Mexico, leads his congregation in ministering to broken and battered women. He writes:

> The very nature of God, expressed directly in his self-revelation in the Scripture, and observed indirectly through his creation, is one of unity. From the indescribable magnificence of the Trinity down to the most basic of all matter, the atom, we see unity; we see purposeful, designed unity.
>
> On the human level, the pursuit of unity which most glorifies God is the oneness between a man and a woman united in marriage—the two becoming one. Nothing else on earth can compete favorably with this graphic visual aid in describing the unity God offers and wants with us.
>
> It is for this reason that when a spouse, typically the husband, fractures this unity through violence, it is the very essence of God's character which is being assaulted. The victim is left powerless, broken, and bereft of that very thing all people crave above all else—unity. Alone, in physical pain, frequently destitute, in fear of

death, doubting that God even exists, the abused woman is often incapable of taking care of herself and her children.[3]

Chapter 4 explores answers to the question most commonly asked of all victims of domestic violence: Why does she stay?

Notes

1. Mary Susan Miller, *No Visible Wounds: Identifying Non-Physical Abuse of Women by Their Men* (New York: Fawcett Columbine, 1995), 32.
2. American College of Emergency Physicians, "Guidelines for the Role of EMS Personnel in Domestic Violence," 2000. http://www.acep.org/webportal/PracticeResources/issues/pubhlth/ violence/GuidelinesRoleEMSPersonnelDomesticViolence.htm (accessed July 11, 2007).
3. From the foreword, *Pastor's Guide—Dealing with Domestic Violence* (Elmhurst, IL: FOCUS Ministries, Inc., 2005), n.p.

Why Does She Stay?

When you ask "Why does she stay?" you lose sight of the crime and place blame on the victim. Why not ask "What's wrong with that man? What can we do to get her to safety and him into a treatment program?"

—Pastor's Guide—Dealing with Domestic Violence[1]

When encountering a victim of domestic violence, the first thing many people ask is "Why does she put up with it? Why doesn't she just leave?" The question is problematic—even while it is also a good question. The fact that we include a chapter with the question as title underscores the legitimacy of the query. Answering the question is critical if we are to understand the heart and mind of the victim sufficiently to give her the long-term help and support she needs.

However, when this question is the first response to an encounter with a victim, the question becomes part of the problem. By asking this question, people place blame on the victim (implicitly suggesting the responsibility is hers to *avoid* the violence) instead of taking action as an individual, a church, or a community to intervene and stop the violent behavior itself. Even our language in reporting domestic violence cases in the media or in personal interaction suggests women are at fault when we say, "Joan was abused by her husband," instead of saying "Tim beats his wife." Few people ask, "What's wrong with that man?" (We will ask it— and offer some ministry-oriented answers in chapter 5.)

CHAPTER 4

Answering the Question

In the 1920s the answer given to "Why doesn't she just leave?" was that battered women were of low intelligence or mentally retarded. In the 1940s the accepted belief was that women did not leave because they were masochistic. By the 1970s experts claimed a woman stayed in an abusive situation because she was isolated from friends and neighbors, had few economic resources, and was terrorized into a state of learned helplessness by repeated abuse.

Throughout the decades, researchers have spent time, energy, and government grants studying women and their problems. But by asking "Why do women stay?" they managed to blame the victims instead of doing anything to stop violent male behavior.

The fact is that many women do leave, and they risk their lives doing so. A woman may leave an average of seven times—leaving and going back home—before she leaves for good. There are many reasons why a woman stays in an abusive relationship or returns home after leaving, but the primary motivation is *fear*.

Fear

The victim has every reason to be afraid. Many abusers threaten to take the children if she leaves—either by accusing her of being an incompetent parent and gaining custody or by kidnapping them. In extreme cases, he may kill them as the ultimate revenge against his wife.

She also fears for her own safety. She may get killed herself! A woman is at 75 percent greater risk of harm from her abuser when she leaves.[2] One abuser threatened to kill his wife, saying "If I can't have you, nobody else will either." In another incident the abuser disfigured his wife's face with acid, proclaiming "Now no one will ever want to look at you again."

Guilt

Religious beliefs and guilt keep many women from leaving abusive situations. They fear the condescending and judgmental reactions of friends and family who believe she is responsible for breaking up the family by leaving. She may also fear offending

God and her church family. Most women who have children try to protect them from the trauma of divorce by staying in an abusive marriage. They do not realize their children will suffer more long-lasting trauma by being in an abusive home than in a single-parent home. Women may not realize that leaving does not necessarily lead to divorce. In some cases, separation is the wake-up call that causes her husband to seek help.

Confusion

Confusion and "crazy making" keep many women off balance and unable to make rational decisions. One day he worships her and places her on a pedestal. The next day she doesn't meet his expectations and falls from grace. The fall is a long one, and she can't understand why he has changed from a loving, generous husband into a maniacal bully who delights in punishing her.

False Hope

False hope distorts a woman's view of reality. Many women stay in an abusive home because they love their husbands and long to see their marriage succeed. They simply want the disrespect and violence to stop. She believes if she tries a little harder or waits a little longer things will change. She believes him when he says the abuse will never happen again. Because he has been wounded in the past, she thinks he needs extra love and care, and she thinks that helping him become whole is her responsibility. Because she loves him, she denies the reality that he is capable of seriously hurting or killing her. False hope convinces her that she needs to protect her husband—even from himself.

Financial Instability

Financial dependence and fear of the unknown paralyze many women as they wonder how they will be able to support themselves and in many cases their children. Most women face financial, social, and emotional hardships when they leave, and they often find that assistance is limited or not available to them. Weak criminal justice systems offer no hope and have failed victims again and again, causing women to be terrified of possibly losing custody of their children and becoming destitute financially. When a woman's life is bound up in her family, she worries about continuing important relationships with stepchildren, grandchildren, in-laws, and friends. She believes her identity will be lost if she leaves.

Lack of Information

Ignorance of the facts and of the consequences of domestic violence causes women to view themselves as the problem rather than understanding the cause of violence is within the heart and mind of the abuser. They believe his violence is caused by temporary problems based on outside circumstances, such as stress at work. Having this mindset, they believe that once the stress is relieved the beatings will stop. In addition, some women are unaware that spousal abuse is spiritually and morally wrong.

Post-Traumatic Stress Disorder (PTSD)

Although most often associated with survivors of war and other violent circumstances, PTSD is not uncommon among women who have been or are abused. It affects the way a person thinks, acts, and behaves. After long periods of trauma and repeated abuse, the victim believes she is helpless and lacks the power to make choices. She may experience flashbacks or nightmares about past abuse and may develop unhealthy coping skills.

Next Question . . .

Having established an extensive list of the obstacles that keep a victim in an abusive environment, the next question is, "How does she finally bring herself to leave?" Women escape an abusive situation through various means and motives, which include the following:

- She believes another abusive episode is inevitable, which this time may be fatal. He has threatened her life and this time she believes he is serious.
- He has refused to seek help, and his violence seems to be escalating.

- She is on the brink of losing her sanity and has to do something before she goes over the edge.
- She hears him telling friends and family lies about her, accusing her of being the one who is threatening him, and claiming to be the victim.
- She finds evidence of sexual perversion or criminal activity.
- He has begun to abuse the children verbally, physically, or sexually.
- She has done everything humanly possible to preserve the marriage, but the situation has worsened instead of improving.
- She hears of other women who have left and this gives her hope.
- She has received promises of support from family members or friends. Someone has become her anchor in the storm.[3]

Instead of asking women why they stay or blaming them for breaking up the family when they leave, their faith community should be asking, "What can we do to help? How can we make the violence stop?" Let's stop blaming the victim and begin holding the abuser accountable.

The next chapter examines the mind of an abuser, looking beneath the charming exterior to a mindset of entitlement and superiority and a desperate need for power and control. Discovering the roots and foundation of abusive thinking can help pastoral counselors understand that behavior modification without transformation of the mind and heart will not produce lasting results.

Notes

1. Brenda Branson and Paula Silva, "Signs of Abuse—Why Do Women Stay?" *Pastor's Guide—Dealing with Domestic Violence* (Elmhurst, IL: FOCUS Ministries, Inc., 2005), n.p.
2. Margo Wilson and Martin Daly, "Spousal Homicide Risk and Estrangement," *Violence & Victims* 8 (1993): 3–16.
3. Adapted from Brenda Branson and Paula Silva, *Manual on Domestic Violence* (Elmhurst, IL: FOCUS Ministries, Inc., 2004).

CHAPTER 5

Inside the Mind of an Abuser

An abuser is a human being, not an evil monster, but he has a profoundly complex and destructive problem that should not be underestimated.

—Lundy Bancroft, *Why Does He Do That?*[1]

Sam has several academic degrees, including a PhD. To his coworkers, Sam appears to be a mild-mannered, highly intelligent man who treats others with respect and kindness. But behind closed doors, Sam frequently beats and kicks his wife, leaving multiple contusions; spits on her in contempt; and screams for her to go stand in the middle of the roadway so she will get hit by a car and die. When an intelligent man acts like a madman, what is going on in his mind?

Ben is the pastor of a thriving church in the city. His congregation keeps growing as people flock to hear his creative, powerful sermons. People are amazed at his compassion and humility as he ministers to the needs of the community. At home Ben constantly criticizes his wife and treats her with disrespect. If dinner is not up to his standards, he pushes the plate onto the floor and demands that she clean up the mess. He requires absolute submission and punishes her if she does not respond quickly enough to meet his needs. What lies in the heart of a man who claims to love God in public but acts like the devil at home?

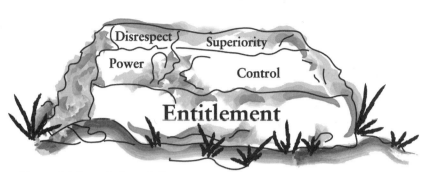

Figure 5.1 Foundation of Abuse

Illustration by Sarah Rebecca Bennett, Hanson, KY. Copyright © 2007 by FOCUS Ministries, Inc.

What is different in the heart and mind of an abusive man compared to a nonabusive man? Although a complicated problem that manifests in a variety of symptoms, the answer can be best understood if reduced to three main elements that form the foundation of all abuse: entitlement, power and control, and disrespect and superiority.

Entitlement

The first foundational element, entitlement, is the mindset of a man who expects to receive special treatment. Even though he has done nothing to deserve it, he expects to receive what he wants because it is his "right" as a man. He sees his rights, opinions, and desires as more important than those of his wife or children. He is so preoccupied with getting his needs met (narcissistic) that he feels misunderstood, not wrong. In extreme cases, he views his wife and children as his property with no rights of their own, which entitles him to treat them as he pleases.

The attitude of entitlement gives an abusive man permission to do whatever it takes to keep his wife and children in line, even if it involves violence. He does not feel guilty for mistreating them, because in his mind he is simply sticking up for his rights. He usually has unrealistic expectations and demands absolute obedience. He threatens or carries out some form of punishment if his demands are not met to his standard of perfection.

Examples of entitlement include the following:

- His opinions are right in his own eyes (Proverbs 12:15), and he expects his wife to agree with him or to remain silent if she disagrees. He gets angry or violent if she expresses a different opinion or expresses concern about his behavior.
- In his distorted interpretation of Scripture he finds the right to rule over his household and make unilateral decisions. Instead of assuming the role of servant leader, as Jesus exemplified, he becomes master and commander while his wife and children become servants and slaves under his dominion.
- He expects the house to be clean, the children to be quiet, and dinner to be on the table as soon as he arrives home from work. He gives himself permission to rest in front of the TV while his wife is expected to take care of his needs and maintain the rest of the household, regardless of whether she is tired or ill. He does not feel equally responsible for household chores or for child care.
- He allows himself freedom to pursue career goals, choose a church, or engage in social events, but she is not allowed the same freedoms without his permission. Her opinion about his choices is either minimized or silenced.
- He spends money as he desires, but she must get his permission—sometimes even for ordinary expenditures. He may dole out a weekly allowance and require her to provide receipts for all purchases.
- He expects her to meet his sexual needs on demand and does not regard forced sexual intercourse with his wife as rape.
- He disregards rules and laws against battery, trespassing, rape, and other abusive behaviors as if they don't apply to him, because he believes he has the right to do what he wants with his "property." If he believes she is disrespectful, he feels entitled to punish her.
- He feels entitled to instant forgiveness if he expresses remorse for violent behavior or for an extramarital affair, even though his remorse is usually short-lived and doesn't result in a lasting change in his behavior. He demands forgiveness for himself but cannot or will not forgive her for similar offenses toward him.

Examples of entitlement are as diverse as the background, culture, and mindset of the abuser. Although male entitlement plays a huge role in wife abuse, not all men who feel entitled are physically abusive. Religious or moral views against violence, a greater respect for women in general, or fear of punishment may inhibit some men from acting out their feelings of entitlement through violence. Although some men find it repugnant to hit a woman, they may consider it normal behavior to use coercion or other more "acceptable" ways to manipulate or discipline their wives when they get out of line—strategies that all too readily fall into the category of emotional or verbal abuse. Remember: the defining line of abuse is when a person establishes a pattern of behavior using power and control to instill fear or inflict harm on someone else in pursuit of one's own desires.

Power and Control

This pair of foundational elements, power and control, drives abusive behavior. When joined with entitlement, they become powerful forces in an abuser's mind, giving him the right to speak or act in any way necessary to gain and maintain control over his wife and children. An abuser acts abusively because he can (with little if any consequence or loss) and because it works. He may feel that he must control her so that she won't control him. By wielding power and control, a man gains certain benefits:

• *He feels important and powerful.* Due to feelings of powerlessness or due to abuse as a child, a man may bolster feelings of insecurity or low self-esteem by "lording it over" his wife and children. Other men have an arrogant, overinflated, narcissistic view of themselves, which, combined with feelings of entitlement, drives them to exert dominion over others who are, in their view, subservient. Ruling over someone else gives them a satisfying feeling that creates a heady rush of significance and power.

• *He gets what he wants.* Control can mean monitoring a woman's thoughts and activities and turning her into a puppet, or it may mean making sure she is left alone and not told what to do. By exerting control through intimidation or violence, his needs and desires become the center of attention. If she does not immediately comply, he uses various tactics to force compliance, such as intimidation, verbal attacks, isolation from friends and family, using the children as weapons, economic control, coercion and threats, spiritual authority, or physical violence. Another benefit of power and control, beyond fulfilling his immediate needs, is being able to silence her from expressing an opinion or having a voice to tell anyone.

• *He is not held accountable for his actions.* Exerting physical force or extreme verbal and emotional abuse on his wife often instills in her a fear of retaliation if she were to take a stand against abusive behavior. Therefore, he does not suffer any consequences for his actions, and he blames her for any problems or frustrations he experiences.

• *He appears strong and in charge to his peers,* who may support attitudes of entitlement or domination. An abuser often chooses a church that embraces the "right" of a husband to rule over his family rather than become a servant leader. He aligns himself with friends who have similar attitudes of superiority and entitlement. This group of supporters invites his ridicule of and complaints about his wife and encourages him to "keep her in her place" as his right and duty.

Superiority and Disrespect

An attitude of superiority and a deep disrespect for women, combined with feelings of entitlement and desire for power and control, prevent the abusive man from feeling empathy or compassion toward his wife. He feels little or no remorse when he slaps her around because in his eyes she is always wrong: she is the one to blame. His goal is to discredit her, to silence her protests, and to divert attention from his bad behavior to her failures.

Where do these attitudes originate? They typically result from (1) male role models in the home who disrespect or abuse women; (2) cultural attitudes toward women as servants or property; and (3) distortion of Scripture preached from pulpits of all denominations for generations, erroneously teaching that because God created Adam first (according to Genesis 2:18-22, the second of two creation accounts), man must be superior to woman in every way—mentally, physically, and spiritually. The colloquial corruption of the King James Version's "help meet" in Genesis 2:18 into the so-called "helpmate" of tradition has been the source of many disrespectful attitudes toward women by Christian men. What the King James translates, "And the LORD God said, It is not good that the man should be alone; I will make him an *help meet* for him," is rendered more clearly in most modern translations as a "suitable helper"—or in the New King James Version as a "helper *comparable* to him" (italics added).

According to Hebrew scholars, the words *help meet* comes from the word *'ezer* (life saver) and *kenegdo* (alongside). Throughout passages in Deuteronomy 33:26, 29 and several instances in the Psalms, the same word *ezer* is used to refer to God as our "help" or "helper." Eve was not designed to be a doormat or servant to Adam—she was his equal ("comparable" in NKJV; "his partner" in the NRSV), an image bearer revealing God's mercy, inviting relationship, and becoming a lifesaving helper alongside Adam.

God does not give husbands the right to control or punish their wives. In fact, this is contrary to God's nature. All throughout the Scriptures, God gives people free will. "I have set before you life and death, blessing and cursing; therefore choose life, that both you and your descendants may live; that you may love the Lord your God, that you may obey His voice, and that you may cling to Him, for He is your life and the length of your days" (Deuteronomy 30:19-20, NKJV).

Other Scripture passages about submission (such as Ephesians 5:21-32) have been distorted and misused by abusive men against their wives. They ignore the foundation of submission in verse 21 ("be subject to one another," NRSV) and focus solely on certain words in verses 22-23 ("wives, submit to your own husbands" and "husband is head of the wife," NKJV) without putting the verses in context with the rest of the chapter, where husbands are instructed to love their wives as Christ loved the church. What does that love and leadership look like? Christ's love did not exploit, exert power and control, intimidate, demean, verbally abuse, or use force or violence. He did not exact punishment or oppression on those who failed to live up to his standards. He did not demand his rights. Instead, he humbled himself as a servant and washed their feet.

Submission is not a right given to a husband to demand but a precious gift given willingly by a woman "as unto the Lord" (Ephesians 5:22, KJV). When an abusive, power-hungry man demands submission as his right, it is no longer a loving gift but a stolen treasure gained by extortion and coercion.

Disrespect for women has many faces, some of which are well-masked by charm, gentleness, quietness, spirituality, and verbal support of women's causes. Disrespect rears its ugly head in the form of jokes about women being inferior to men and sexual talk that demeans and objectifies women. Even nonviolent men show disrespect by devaluing a woman's opinion, by being critical and sarcastic, by dismissing her needs or desires, and by exhibiting an attitude of entitlement and superiority. One loving family man, a well-respected leader in his church, admitted anonymously, "If I woke up one morning and found that God had turned me into a woman, I'd kill myself."

Men who feel entitled show violent disrespect to a woman by spitting on her with contempt; screaming, raging or cursing; destroying personal property; injuring or killing her pets; undermining her role as a parent; forcing her to engage in sexual activity distasteful to her; slamming the car door on her hand or running over her foot; refusing to allow her to get medical treatment or to purchase adequate clothing and necessities; or causing her physical harm. As we have already established in previous chapters, these examples are just a few of the many atrocities against women happening every day behind closed doors—carried out by men in our neighborhoods and churches who are convinced they are *entitled* to do so.

Demanding a change in behavior or requiring attendance in an anger management class alone cannot solve this complex problem, because a solid foundation of entitlement, power and control, and superiority and disrespect has been firmly laid in the hearts and minds of abusive men. According to Lundy Bancroft, author of *Why Does He Do That?* and an expert who has worked with angry, controlling men for more than fifteen years, the problem is embedded in what a man thinks rather than what he feels. Understanding this truth can help dispel many of the myths that confuse pastors and counselors who may look for and focus on surface symptoms, which can be more easily diagnosed and fixed, rather than on the deeper issues of the soul.

Many misperceptions so popular today have been created by the abuser himself as a smokescreen to prevent another person from digging too deeply into his heart and mind. He is a master of manipulation who will use a myriad of excuses and blame to distract anyone trying to get at the heart of the matter. Here are a few common myths that abusers use to divert attention from the real problem:

Myth: **She did something to provoke him.**

Truth: Victims of violence should not be held responsible for their own assault. By blaming the victim, responsibility shifts from the abuser. The question no longer is "Why did John hit Julie?" but becomes "What did Julie do to provoke him?" In the workplace, John deals with frustration and provocation every day. Does he assault his coworkers when they push his buttons? Dig deeper beneath the surface excuse of being provoked to uncover the likelihood that John chose to assault Julie because of his deep-rooted attitude of superiority, feeling of entitlement, and desperate need to maintain power and control. Since most abusers thrive on creating confusion, blaming the victim is usually his first strategic move to divert the attention away from himself.

Myth: **He has a problem controlling his anger.**

Truth: Anger is often a part of abusive behavior, but it is not the primary cause. Abusive attitudes of entitlement, superiority, and control breed anger when a man does not get his way. Does he control his anger at work, at church, or in social settings when someone disagrees with him? Probably so. His target is usually at home, and even then he controls how far he will allow his temper to rage, sometimes by calculating to what extent he can frighten or injure his wife without getting caught or looking bad to other people. Is a man truly out of control when he chooses the places on his wife's body to beat black and blue—bruises that will be hidden by clothing when she goes to work or to church? The truth is not that he loses control of himself but that he takes control over her by becoming angry and violent.

Myth: **He has emotional or mental problems because he grew up in an abusive home.**

Truth: A flawed value system and abusive experiences in the childhood home may lay the foundation for subsequent abusive behavior. Certainly a man may learn distorted beliefs about Scripture, about women, about sex, and about relationships from a dysfunctional or abusive family, and those early experiences may contribute to his behaviors in adulthood. However, a bad childhood alone does not cause a man to become abusive; many men who have experienced or witnessed abuse as a child make a choice not to repeat the cycle of abuse in their own homes. Conversely, not all abusers were victims of abuse themselves.

Myth: **If he would stop drinking or taking drugs, the violence would stop.**

Truth: Even though substance abuse aggravates the symptoms of domestic violence, it does not cause it. The National Coalition Against Domestic Violence puts it succinctly: "Domestic violence and drug and alcohol addiction frequently occur together but are two separate and distinct problems. *One does not cause the other.*"[2] Therefore, attendance at Alcoholics Anonymous or recovery groups may benefit the drug or alcohol problem but does not cure or break up the foundation of an abusive mindset. These issues should be addressed using separate treatment programs.

Many other beliefs, beyond the ones glimpsed at here, are at work in the mind of an abuser and influence his behavior. But most of them are based on the foundation of entitlement, power and control, and attitudes of superiority and disrespect.

How can an abusive man break free from the belief system that entangles his heart and mind? While many good treatment programs around the country can help, the underlying cause is often

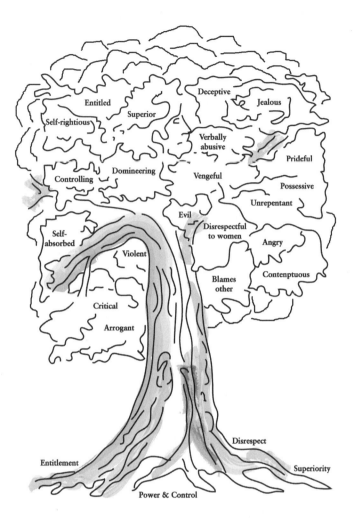

Figure 5.2 The Roots and Fruits of Abuse

Illustration by Sarah Rebecca Bennett, Hanson, KY. Copyright © 2007 by FOCUS Ministries, Inc., 2006.]

missed unless the problem is identified and dealt with as a spiritual issue. Chapter 11 deals more fully with these spiritual issues, which originated with the first violent man—Cain.

Let's be clear: The abusive man is not a monster. Rather, he has become his own god who trusts in his own heart (Proverbs 28:26), insulates himself with self-protective strategies to prevent pain, and has convinced himself he is always right (Proverbs 12:15). The only antidote for a hardened, self-obsessed heart is transformation of the mind (Romans 12:2), which can be found only through an encounter with Jesus Christ. This is not just a one-time encounter that many churches call a salvation experience but an ongoing relationship for a lifetime and for all eternity.

As an image bearer of God, each man has a choice to grow the roots of his life deep into the soil of faith, grace, and truth. He can become like the tree planted by rivers of water (Psalm 1:3) who thrives and brings forth good fruit. A man who allows his heart to be hardened through the deceit of the enemy and his own foolishness, however, will develop a root system (a foundation, to return to the metaphor of Figure 5.1) from which the fruit of abuse will grow.

Notes

1. Lundy Bancroft, *Why Does He Do That? Inside the Minds of Angry and Controlling Men* (New York: Penguin Putnam, 2002), 112.
2. "Domestic Violence and Substance Abuse Facts," National Coalition Against Domestic Violence. http://www.ncadv.org/files/substanceabuse.pdf (accessed July 11, 2007).

Effects of Family Violence

CHAPTER 6

Children are treasures from the Lord to be
protected at all costs. That responsibility
belongs to all of us—not just their parents!

—*FOCUS Newsletter,* February 2003

When the seeds of disrespect and violence are sown in the hearts of children, what harmful effects will grow and take root in their lives? How will the harvest of abuse affect their future marriages and children?

Most people would agree that children benefit from and even need a father's love and influence. We hear words of caution from many sources about the trauma of divorce and the challenges for children living in a single-parent home. However, the long-lasting effects of family violence are much more damaging to a child than living with just one parent. When someone says, "An abusive father is better than no father at all," that person is significantly misguided and has no idea what living in the chaos of an abusive home is like.

Tony grew up in a church-going family and attended a Christian school for most of his adolescence. He attended a Bible club as a youngster, was active in the youth group at church, and attended church twice on Sundays each week with his parents. Tony's dad was involved in every aspect of his life—from attending soccer games to hosting huge parties for Tony and his friends. He even introduced them to famous people, including U.S. presidents and movie stars. From outward appearances, Tony had a loving family and an idyllic childhood. Behind closed doors, life was confusing and unstable, often violent and dangerous. As a young man in his midtwenties, Tony described some of the memories and lessons he learned from his dad:

> Dad, when I was just a toddler, I listened carefully as you blamed Mom whenever you didn't get what you wanted. I learned a lot from you as I repeated your words to visitors in our home, explaining with contempt that it was Mom's fault when our house was messy. You also taught me that it is okay to lie, cheat, and steal whenever it served your purposes. Remember the toys, balls, and sports equipment we took from apartment courtyards and soccer fields? You said it was okay because some irresponsible person had left them there.
>
> You took me to church every Sunday and taught me to be religious. You encouraged me to take my Bible to church, but we didn't ever read it during the week except when you quoted some passages to put Mom 'in her place' and let her know you were the boss. You taught me to communicate with God only at mealtimes. I never heard you pray, except when you said 'Oh my God' if you were upset or startled.
>
> I remember when you told me that women couldn't be trusted. You warned me not to let my mother control me. I learned from you that women need to be put in their place from time to time, and if you lose your temper and hit them, it is really their fault because they provoked you. You taught me how to use my voice to intimidate women by speaking loudly with a bit of sarcasm and a hint of a threat. It makes women afraid and puts you in control. It's easy to reduce a woman to tears by telling her how ugly and incompetent she is. It certainly worked on Mom!
>
> You also taught me how to intimidate men. Remember how you threatened those men who confronted you about how you were mistreating Mom? Whenever grown men came face to face with your piercing eyes, raised fist, intimidating voice, subtle threats to harm their family, and not-so-subtle threats to sue them for harassment, they usually backed off and left you alone.
>
> Dad, I looked up to you and wanted to be just like you . . . until you began treating me just like you treated Mom. Dad, I love you, but I do not want to be like you. You have taught me many

lessons that I am working hard to unlearn. Mom deserved a better life and so did I. I've made the decision to stop the cycle of abuse with me so my son won't be ashamed to call me his father and my wife won't live in fear and humiliation.

Witnessing Violence

Each year more than 3 million children are exposed to violence in their homes.[1] Many children who witness violence in the home demonstrate significant behavior and/or emotional problems. Children can be adversely affected just by overhearing arguments, even when physical violence is not present. According to Dr. Richard Gelles, a leader in the study of domestic violence, the worst thing that can happen to children is to grow up in an abusive home.[2]

When children grow up experiencing or witnessing violence, they react in various ways, depending on age and gender. (Refer to Appendix A, pages 123–124, for a list of effects of abuse on various age groups and the ways children are drawn into the chaos.) Some children react to family violence by internalizing their feelings, which manifests as depression and anxiety. In young children, depression may take the form of sadness, poor appetite, chronic fatigue, withdrawal from friends, and low self-esteem. One child told his mother, "Even when I look happy on the outside, I am really sad on the inside."

Aggressive, angry behavior is a common reaction to witnessing family violence. Many young people use anger and aggressive behavior to cope with their fear. Others use alcohol, drugs, sex, or food to numb their feelings. An older child threatening or abusing younger siblings to get what he or she wants is not uncommon behavior. A son may become physically and verbally abusive toward his mother.

Exposure to Verbal and Emotional Violence

Children who have witnessed physical abuse often report that they were more traumatized by emotional and verbal abuse. Effects of emotional and verbal abuse include sudden speech disorders;

overreacting to mistakes (becoming perfectionists); chronic anxiety; self-put-downs ("I'm so stupid"); and repetitive behaviors such as hair twisting, nail biting, rocking, cutting themselves with razor blades, and bed-wetting. Children may relive episodes of violence through dreams or by watching TV.

Some children may become overprotective of a parent or become a parent's caretaker or confidant. Some of these symptoms may not become apparent until the child gets older. One young man in his early twenties finally admitted that his father had constantly put him down for the way he wrote his name. Every time he signed his name on a letter, check, or legal document, he was reminded of his father's disapproval.

Through a Child's Eyes

Even though a parent tells a child "It is not your fault," the child often assumes guilt and blame for the abusive parent's behavior. Here are some thoughts seen through the eyes of a child:

- It's my fault. I did something wrong.
- If I were prettier or if I acted better, Dad would not get upset.
- I'm afraid of my dad. Sometimes he gets so angry I'm afraid he will hurt me again.
- What if my dad hurts my mom so badly she can't take care of me?
- Why doesn't my mom protect me? Why doesn't she leave and take me with her?
- I'm mad at God. I prayed for him to make my dad stop being mean and God didn't answer my prayers.
- If my heavenly Father is anything like my dad, I don't want anything to do with God.

Lessons Learned in an Abusive Home

- *They learn to keep secrets.* Children are told not to tell anyone what is said or done in the home and often threatened with physical harm if they talk. Some are told they will be taken away from their parents if they tell anyone.

- *They learn that violence is an acceptable way to solve problems* or to get what they want. Boys grow up thinking a man has the right "to keep his wife in line," even if doing so includes violence.
- *They believe abuse is normal.* Children believe the myth that all families experience abuse. Girls grow up accepting abuse from boyfriends or husbands as normal and believing it is their role to take it.
- *They learn not to trust people.* Children grow up believing people who claim to love them will hurt them. So they build a wall of self-protection from painful relationships.
- *They learn to take on additional responsibilities* to protect their parents and siblings who are being abused. Children work hard to keep the peace and pacify the abuser. They often feel guilty and blame themselves for violence in the home. They believe the lie that if they were better children, their father would not get upset and become violent.

Rico grew up in an abusive home. He witnessed all forms of domestic violence against his mother and experienced verbal, emotional, and physical abuse from his dad, who claimed to love him. Each time Rico's dad hurled verbal missiles or assaulted him physically, Rico maintained self-control and refrained from hitting back or returning evil for evil. Through the years, Rico internalized the anger he did not allow himself to direct toward his dad—until his eighteenth birthday. This is the letter Rico sent to his dad as a declaration of his independence from eighteen years of living in what everyone else perceived to be a wonderful Christian home:

Don't worry. You haven't been robbed. Now that I am eighteen years old, I've been making a lot of decisions, but this was by far the biggest. You will notice that all my stuff is gone. . . . I will no longer need it at your house, because I will not be returning here ever again. Not on Tuesdays, not on Thursdays, not every other weekend.

Please do not assume this to be some stupid stage or a spiteful action due to the recent arguments we've had concerning prom. Oh no. The past several years have been leading to this. We had good times, but there was a darker side. Do you remember grabbing me by my throat one day in the back doorway? Let me tell you what I remember. I remember being sent to my room to play so you and mom could 'have a talk.' And while I sat there playing *Batman*, I can remember you screaming your &*#@&*# head off at my mother for trivial things that no one in their right mind would care about. I remember you grabbing her at my soccer game. I got on the witness stand and lied under oath to protect you, but I saw you do it. I saw the bruises you left on her. I remember you carrying me out of my mom's house kicking and screaming because I was so sure you were going to kidnap me.

When I look back at my life, I don't see the good times at parks or watching *Batman*. I remember the evil inside of you, the evil that hurt me. This is the end. From this day forth, I walk the earth fatherless. Do not try to contact me in any way. I would like to leave you with this thought: eight years ago your wife left you. Now your son is leaving you. Do you ever wonder what is so bad about you that no one wants to be near you? If you haven't, you should start. And when you find out what it is, I would suggest getting help for your sake, and for the sake of those left around you. Get help. Goodbye.

Everyone in an abusive home has been wounded—the abuser during childhood, the victim at present, and the children for a lifetime. Instead of learning to become a whole, integrated person, a child's thinking may be twisted to model the father's manipulation and domination. The abuser's children carry the baggage of guilt and anger that impacts their future employers, friends, spouse, and children. As long as abuse continues and the abuser is not held accountable, the abuser's children are set up for a lifetime of destructive patterns and failed marriages.

Teen-Dating Violence

Boys who witness their dad's violence toward their mom are more likely to repeat the pattern in their dating relationships and marriages. The message that a man has a right to keep his woman in line becomes ingrained at an early age. Girls grow up believing disrespect is normal, and they may either tolerate it from a boyfriend or spouse or they may end up being an abusive spouse themselves.

Dating violence is a real and serious danger—one that is increasing in frequency in nearly every area.[3] A study done by Liz Claiborne, Inc., indicates that verbal and sexual abuse among teens is escalating through the use of technology—via instant messaging, social networking sites such as MySpace, and cell phone text messaging.[4] Studies now indicate that one in every five teens has been the victim of physical dating violence (slapping, punching, pushing, kicking, or choking), and nearly one in three teens reports *knowing* a peer who has been a victim.[5] Although most dating violence victims are female, young men are also victims of abusive girlfriends, many of whom use emotional and verbal abuse to control and intimidate.

Many teenagers interpret a partner's possessiveness and violent behavior as a sign of love. They have either seen violence as a way of life at home or they have not been taught about healthy relationships. Dating violence not only includes physical abuse but also verbal and emotional abuse. It often takes the form of obsession and possessiveness. A girl may be expected to give up all other friendships—especially with other boys—and extracurricular activities, such as sports, music, and church groups, to spend all free time with her boyfriend. He may give her a pager or cell phone so he can check in with her several times a day to monitor her activities.

Meredith, a fourteen-year-old in the ninth grade, talked to her controlling boyfriend on the phone seven or eight times each night. Her mother overheard her hysterically begging for forgiveness and pledging her love to him over and over. After a fight with her boyfriend, Meredith tried to commit suicide, thinking that would get his attention.

Joy finally broke up with her abusive boyfriend when she realized the relationship was becoming more violent. One day when she was visiting the home of her best friend, her boyfriend called and threatened to kill her and her friend's family if she did not reconcile with him. Instead of calling the police or asking her parents for help, Joy agreed to get back together with him.

To help teens trapped in the clutches of dating violence, parents need to be on the alert for danger signs. Teens need to learn how to recognize the red flags of abusive behavior so that they can avoid unhealthy relationships. (See Appendix A for "Red Flags for Parents and Teens," a checklist to help identify teen-dating violence.) To develop open communication with their teens, parents must provide a safe, nonjudgmental atmosphere. They must practice effective listening without overreacting or giving looks of disapproval. Wise parents will acknowledge their child's feelings and establish the facts before launching into a torrent of advice.

Although the temptation to issue ultimatums to discontinue abusive relationships will be strong, parents will find it more productive to keep talking and monitoring the situation unless the teen is in a life-threatening situation. When a girl's safety is at risk and her boyfriend does not respect restraining orders or other forms of intervention, her parents are faced with making extreme decisions such as relocating across the country to protect their child.

Parents can be the lifeline for their children, especially when a girl is ready to break up with her abusive boyfriend. The decision to break up is difficult not only because of the emotional upheaval but also because the breakup is the most dangerous time in an abusive relationship. Parents can and should help their daughter develop a safety plan to prepare for the boyfriend's reaction and possible harassment. Together, they can identify safe places where she can go if she can't get home, people who can accompany her going to and from school, people to call in a crisis, and how to handle medical emergencies.

Teen Dating Statistics

Teen-dating violence runs across race, gender, and socioeconomic lines. Victims are both male and female but boys and girls are abusive in different ways. "Girls are more likely to yell, threaten to hurt themselves, pinch, slap, scratch, or kick. Boys injure girls more and are more likely to punch their partner and force them to participate in unwanted sexual activity."[6]

- Eighty-one percent of parents surveyed either believe teen-dating violence is not an issue or admit they don't know if it is an issue.[7]

- A slight majority of teens (54 percent) express willingness to admit dating violence to their parents, but an overwhelming 73 percent would confide in a friend.[8]
- Reports of physical abuse (hitting, punching, slapping, etc.) in dating relationships is roughly equal among boys (10 percent) and girls (12 percent), but girls report injury (bruise, etc.) more often.[9]
- Fifty percent of youth reporting both dating violence and rape also reported attempting suicide, compared to 12.5 percent of nonabused girls and 5.4 percent of nonabused boys.[10]

For parents, teachers, and church leaders to react to dating violence when it occurs is not enough. Proactive steps must be taken to teach young people how to respect themselves and others and how to tell the difference between healthy and abusive relationships. When so many children in today's world suffer the consequences of violence, broken homes, and a distorted view of how women should be treated, the church needs to speak up loudly and clearly against violence and disrespect. The pastor is the person on the front lines who must take the initiative from the pulpit, followed by every Sunday school teacher and youth leader who trains young minds to follow the example of Jesus and his interactions with others.

The world's standard of love and beauty, the shameful legacy of abusive parents, and the silence of the church have distorted the thinking of this generation and continue a cycle of abuse that must be broken. As parents, grandparents, teachers, pastors, youth leaders, or friends, we must ask ourselves what we can do to help just one child who has been affected by family violence.

Notes

1. American Psychological Association, "Violence and the Family: Report of the APA Presidential Task Force on Violence and the Family," 1996.
2. Richard Gelles, "The Family and Its Role in the Abuse of Children," *Psychiatric Annals* 17 (1987): 229–32.

3. Liz Claiborne, Inc., "Tech Abuse in Teen Relationships Study," (Teen Research Unlimited, 2007): 12. http://www.loveisnotabuse.com/pdf/06-208%20Tech%20 Relationship%20Abuse%20TPL.pdf (accessed July 12, 2007).

4. Ibid., 6–9.

5. Ibid., 12.

6. Teen Victim Project, "Dating Violence," National Center for Victims of Crime. http://www.ncvc.org/tvp/AGP.Net/Components/ DocumentViewer/Download.aspxnz?DocumentID=42857 (accessed July 12, 2007).

7. Liz Claiborne, Inc., "Teen Dating Violence and Social Environment Survey," (Knowledge Networks, 2000). http://www.loveisnotabuse.com/surveyresults_2007mstr.htm (accessed July 12, 2007).

8. Liz Claiborne, Inc., "Teen Relationship Abuse Research," Omnibuzz Topline Findings (Teenage Research Unlimited, 2005): 8.

9. Ibid., 9.

10. D. M. Ackard and D. Neumark-Sztainer, "Date Violence and Date Rape Among Adolescents; Associations with Eating Behaviors and Psychological Health," *Child Abuse or Neglect* 26 (2002): 455–73.

CHAPTER 7

Men as Victims—Women as Perpetrators

One of the most difficult admissions for a man to make is to admit having been beaten by a woman. It is not natural. It is not manly. And the shame that one feels . . . no one can describe the shame that a man feels.

—Tommy Snow, Domestic Violence Intervention Facilitator[1]

A phone conversation we will never forget took place just as we finished a radio broadcast on family violence toward women. The voice on the phone was clearly not a woman but a young man with a distinctive accent—a student from overseas who was attending a local Bible college. With a quiet, trembling voice he admitted that he was afraid of his wife. The day before when he arrived home from class and walked into the couple's apartment, a knife whizzed through the air, barely missing his right ear and becoming embedded in the wall behind his head. He fled the apartment and slept in his car that night. His plea was heartbreaking. Not only was he in an unfamiliar country but also he was a Bible college student here on a scholarship. Where could he go for help? Who would believe him? How could he get help for his wife?

Research indicates that between 5 and 35 percent of family violence victims are men, but statistics do not present a realistic picture because many cases go unreported. Men are less likely to call the police, because they feel embarrassed or because they may have a difficult time convincing the police they are the victims and not the perpetrators.

Although male perpetrators are capable of doing greater harm to women through physical force, female perpetrators can terrorize their husbands with weapons (including fingernails) and words and through manipulative attitudes of vengeance and emotional blackmail. Why do women do that? The core issues are similar to those addressed in chapter 5—feelings of entitlement and superiority, need for power and control, and unhealed wounds from childhood.

In some cases, however, a woman learns to fight back to defend herself from assault by her husband.[2] She makes the mistake of fighting instead of fleeing, which establishes a behavior pattern that is difficult to break. While she may have been a victim initially, she begins to move back and forth between the role of a victim and perpetrator. Regardless of the motivation for her violent behavior, the new cycle of violence and her participation in a pattern of retaliatory abuse puts her and her family at great risk, and she must be held accountable for her own actions.

Men who are victims of domestic violence cope with it in various ways. They may develop a "fight back" strategy, which often lands them in jail as the perpetrator. Others quietly take whatever is hurled at them (words, weapons, emotional attacks) but develop ulcers, suffer depression or thoughts of suicide, or turn to drugs or alcohol. Some men escape by spending extra time at work, hiding away in their garage or den working on projects, or by developing emotional or sexual relationships with other women.

Men stay in abusive relationships for several reasons:

- They are ashamed to admit they are being abused by a woman. They may face ridicule from their peers and lose the respect of their friends, colleagues, and family.
- They have low self-worth. They may feel they don't deserve a better relationship or aren't capable of finding another partner.
- They compensate for her bad behavior by focusing on the good aspects of the relationship.

- They are concerned about the well-being of the children and may feel better able to protect them if they stay in the home.
- Fewer resources are available to help abused men, such as support groups, shelters, etc.

Finding Support

If a man is being verbally, emotionally, or physically abused by his wife, what should he do? The first step is to tell someone and seek help from a counselor or join a support group. He should encourage his wife to seek professional help or join a batterers treatment program. Regardless of a woman's tirades or assaults, retaliation with verbal or physical abuse is never justified. An abused man should also document all incidents of physical assault and if the police are involved, make sure the police report accurately identifies the perpetrator. If safety is an issue, an abused man should leave his home. In most states, men may also find help by calling the domestic violence coalition hotline in their area. Many shelters accommodate men as well as women. If they do not accommodate men on site, provision is often made for them to stay at a local hotel.

The best way to help a man who is a victim of domestic violence is to listen, validate his story, and let him know he is not alone. Most literature and safety plans for female victims of domestic violence also apply to male victims. After establishing safety, working through the victim's issues of shame and self-esteem is an important role for a pastor or counselor.

Dr. Tommy Snow is an advocate for domestic violence victims and a group facilitator for an abuser treatment program in Georgia. His story illustrates the dynamics of being terrorized by an abusive wife.[3] He says, "One of the most difficult admissions for a man to make is to admit having been beaten by a woman. It is not natural, . . . not manly." and "very fearful, because who knows what response [the admission] will provoke. Will it be support? Laughter? Jeering? . . . No one can describe the shame that a man feels." Snow lived that shame for twelve years until it culminated in a nervous breakdown. Because of the shame and humiliation he felt from the abuse and the subsequent nervous breakdown, he didn't leave his mother's house for three months. Fear kept him there and finally motivated him to leave. One afternoon when his mother returned from church she reported, "'Brother Wiley said that if you do not leave this house, you will *never* leave this house!' I believed what he said, so out of fear I left even though I was afraid."

Snow's own violent response to his wife's abuse compounded his feelings of shame. He admits, "I was no saint either, but I was not physically violent initially. After being struck, scratched, and attacked I retaliated with physical violence. That made my shame and guilt even worse." He understood that his wife's violence was an expression of her internal pain. She "acted out of the pain of being adopted and given away by her natural biological mother, but there were no consequences for her violent behavior, which in turn reinforced the violent behavior itself. She was raised by wonderful people . . . but [they] never meted out any punishment of any type for her behavior, thus, reinforcing it." He recalls an episode, and a turning point for him, that occurred after a group of young people visited them in their home. "After they left, she began slapping and hitting me, telling me how much they loved her. This unprovoked attack did not make sense to me. I believe she was trying to say that people loved her in spite of her behavior. I left after that and stayed away for five months because I could not keep living in such turmoil."

Embarrassment and shame, however, prevented him from seeking help or speaking up. "I did not want it made public that I, a man, was a *victim* of domestic violence. I was truly ashamed and full of pride, and she knew it. I believe she capitalized on it as well. . . . This is probably the main reason many male victims suffer in silence—the humiliation of being beaten by a woman, any woman, especially one with whom you are in an intimate partner relationship. You feel less respected and suffer a loss of your manhood. . . . Many men probably think, like I did, that they will suffer greater humiliation if anyone finds out, so they cover it up. . . . My victimization took place publicly. When our personal identity is torn apart, we see, feel and think differently; and as a result, we also behave differently."

Snow says male victims of abuse can find their way through and out of the violence, shame, fear, and embarrassment to healing. In addition to "the wisdom to seek counseling," their hope lies in allowing "God . . . to execute healing in our lives. We must not lie and continue to hide what happened to us. We must acknowledge the truth concerning the traumatic events of violence and seek the healing power of God."

Finding Resources

Men who suffer the shame and embarrassment of having an abusive spouse need to know they will be believed when they have the courage to share their secret. They need the same practical help and support as women who are being battered by their husbands. Although the need is significant, faith-based resources to help men victimized by an abusive spouse are few. Most domestic violence literature has been developed by women for women. Men who have experienced domestic violence or who have expertise in counseling that addresses domestic violence issues have an opportunity to bridge this gap, developing resources, programs, and support groups for men who need help.

Understanding the dynamics of domestic violence is vital for pastors and counselors so that they can determine how to help these men in need, discerning between a man who is a victim of domestic violence and an abuser who claims to be a victim. Pastors and churches that are developing support programs for women and children who are victims of domestic violence and accountability groups for abusers deserve the community's applause. A further challenge to the body of Christ is to remember that men also suffer silently from verbal, emotional, and physical abuse and need help and spiritual direction as they deal with shame and loss.

Notes

1. From a personal e-mail from Tommy L. Snow, PhD, Domestic Violence Intervention Programs, Genesis 8 LLC, 487 Winn Way, Suite 101, Decatur, GA 30030. Used by permission.
2. While a fight reaction is natural to most human beings when threatened or attacked, we don't advocate such a response. First, it is rarely effective on the stronger abuser, and second, even a fingernail scratch on the perpetrator can be used against the victim when the police arrive. We recommend that the victim leave as soon as it is safe to do so.
3. Quoted and paraphrased from Snow, used by permission.

CHAPTER 8

Terror in the Parsonage

Where could I go? He was abusing me more
and more, but he was my pastor as well as my
husband. I had made a lifelong commitment to
him. He preached one thing and lived another.

—Dee Engel, Yucaipa, CA[1]

When a woman is abused by her pastor-husband, she faces a dilemma much more complicated than that of other victims of domestic violence. Many people look to her husband for spiritual guidance. They also look to her. She may be considered a copastor or the "first lady" of the church. In either role, she is expected to smile and to support her husband wholeheartedly.

In most churches, the pastor is honored as the undershepherd of Christ's flock who is expected to lead the church family closer to God. But what happens when the leader is troubled? Many pastors' wives cover up their husband's affairs or verbal and physical assaults to protect the church, to preserve their husband's reputation, and to protect their only source of income. They describe their husbands as good men who love God and have a great heart for people. One pastor's wife described her husband's passion for preaching the Word as unparalleled in the pulpit, but he used that same zeal at home to terrorize her and their children.

When a pastor is well liked and delivers sermons that stir the hearts and emotions of people, church members have difficulty believing he could be a tyrant at home. If the pastor's wife breaks her silence and tells the truth, she is often not believed. She may be considered a troublemaker or mentally unstable. Many pastors' wives are advised to forgive him and to hang in there because he is under stress and needs her support. One pastor's wife described her Sunday charade of smiling and looking as if everything was okay on the outside when she felt broken and forsaken on the inside.

Dee Engel was a pastor's wife who suffered extreme verbal, emotional, physical, and sexual abuse. The following is her story.[2]

Dee and her husband met during college. They were both "preparing for full-time Christian service," she recalls. "Friends thought we were the ideal couple to work with young people. However, within days of our marriage, I realized I really didn't know the person I had married. Oh, he still made me laugh, and he was still good looking and charming; however, a new and very different person also lived within him. He was controlling and had a fierce temper. His demands sexually were insatiable. He collected all my money and asked for my paychecks as soon as I got them. He yelled at me and slammed doors. Then he hit me across the face."

The abuse—physical, verbal, and sexual—continued while he attended seminary and she worked two jobs to support them. "I was confused, and when I asked what was going on he told me to shut up and be more submissive. I didn't know whom to talk to because we lived hundreds of miles away from my family and most of my friends. He wouldn't allow me to make long-distance phone calls because he said we couldn't afford them. Everyone thought he was fun loving, easygoing, and a wonderful Christian. I was trapped. Inside I was dying." Dee kept her troubles locked inside while she worked hard to change herself to please her husband. "I began to read books on marriage that said I should be sexier and more submissive. I began to think this was God's way of chipping away at my rough edges much like you would polish a diamond."

When he finished seminary they moved to a small town where he served as a pastor. The abuse continued—for twenty-six years. "He . . . was my pastor as well as my husband. I had made a lifelong commitment to him. He preached one thing and lived another." During this time Dee and her husband had two children, and she no longer worked outside the home. The abuse got worse. "He was yelling and swearing more, becoming more angry and sadistic. He began to beat me and told me I deserved to be punished. I wanted to leave him, but I was afraid of what he would do to me and what would happen to the children . . . until one day I got angry enough to do something about it."

She found the strength and the words she needed in Scripture. "I told my husband that my body was a temple of the Holy Spirit, and I was not going to allow him to continue to abuse it any longer. He became furious and . . . told me to get out. I threw my things into suitcases and put them in my car. I freed myself from abuse."

Dee says her "journey to freedom and wholeness was long and painful." She had nowhere to go when she left the house. Another pastor helped her find a safe place to stay and a counselor for the long work of recovery. The pastor assured her that she "had done the right thing." During the next twelve weeks Dee experienced an intense process of allowing herself to face and feel the pain she had learned to deny for so long. For a time her husband's journey included treatment and counseling, but "after a while it became obvious that he was not willing to confess his sin and seek reconciliation." With their friends and at church he told a different story about their relationship.

Dee wanted to retaliate, but she didn't. "Eventually I realized I had to make another decision if I really wanted to heal. I had to forgive him for the wrong he had done to me, even though he never said he was sorry. Otherwise, I would become bitter and stuck in my situation." And she had to give up the dream that they would live together again. She moved to another community where she "could move forward with [her] life." She reflects, "The journey to freedom hasn't always been easy. . . . But God is faithful, and he is all I need."

Many other pastors' wives have similar stories of controlling, abusive husbands who are smooth-tongued orators in the pulpits but at home brutalize their families with scathing words that disrespect and wound those they claim to love. Pastors who abuse their wives may impress their congregations with their knowledge of the Word, but they twist and pervert it to keep their wives in line. One pastor's wife described getting a bitter taste in her mouth every time she heard her husband quote Scripture passages about wives submitting to their husbands because in her house that meant she must become his slave or be beaten as punishment.

For some, the abuse involves extreme psychological abuse. Even sleep offers no refuge when he keeps her up throughout the night with his screaming, ranting and raving, accusations, and threats. His demands are relentless, and he monitors her every move through the use of an electronic tracking device—the cell phone. She may be expected to call him when she leaves the house for any reason and check in every fifteen minutes to give an update of her activities. One woman was overheard talking on the phone with her husband, asking him if she would be allowed a few minutes extra to stop at the grocery store on the way home from work. Throughout the phone call she responded to him with "Yes, sir," and "Yes, master" as she received her instructions from her "warden." His control over her was as effective as if she were wearing an electronic ankle device used by court systems to track criminals.

When psychological control isn't effective, or sometimes in addition to it, the pastor's wife may be beaten with a belt, pummeled with fists, sexually abused, or slapped across the face with the same hand that serves Communion and baptizes in the name of the Father, Son, and Holy Spirit. Yet, the abusive pastor feels no remorse because his mindset of entitlement and superiority gives him permission to keep his wife and children in line. He proclaims Jesus' love from the pulpit but justifies calling his wife a "stupid heifer," or worse, at home. Spiritually, the pastor-abuser is his own god, seeking his own glory.

Why She Stays

Why does a pastor's wife cover for her abusive husband? Why does she endure years of abuse instead of telling someone? In addition to the reasons identified in chapter 4, which apply more widely, here are some reasons a pastor's wife stays in an abusive relationship:

- She feels her husband is God's man and she must not do anything to bring shame to her family or the church. She is a godly woman who prayed for a godly man to marry but found out too late that he does not carry out that godliness in his own home.

- Her goal is the preservation of her family. She thinks that if she can "fix" herself and please her husband, she can save her family. But the more she complies with his demands, the more obsessed he becomes to maintain power and control.

- She does not want to bring disgrace to God or hinder the ministry by exposing her husband's abuse. She desperately tries to be a godly wife by submitting to her husband and keeping his abuse a secret.

- Like most abused women, she is emotionally and financially tied to her husband and afraid of living without him. This dependence is exacerbated for the pastor's wife, however. If she tells the church about the abuse, her husband might lose his job, which would affect the financial stability of the family. If they live in the church parsonage, they may also lose their home.

When the abuse becomes so intolerable, especially when she sees her children suffering, the pastor's wife may reach out to a friend or the elders of the church for help. By this time, she may be sick mentally and physically. The response of the church and close friends may literally save her life. Not only is she at risk by her husband's violent behavior, but she may see suicide or homicide as the only way out. The body of Christ can make all the difference to a pastor's wife who needs refuge from the false shepherd who attacks instead of protects.

How to Help Her

Ways to help a pastor's wife include the following:

- *Believe her.* Since most pastors' wives will go to great lengths to cover for their husbands, realize how much courage it took for her to break her silence and seek help.

- *Don't be sidetracked or sucked in by the abuser's denial* of any wrongdoing or his claim that she is mentally unstable. Remember that he can be very convincing in the pulpit with his knowledge of Scripture, so don't fall for his charming rhetoric, pretentious tears, or victim mentality (he may claim she is the tyrant in the home).

• *Don't sweep the incident under the carpet* and advise her to work things out for the good of the church or for the cause of Christ. Evil needs to be exposed; otherwise it continues to grow and mutate like an insidious cancer. Even though the process will be painful, the church family needs to be aware of the basic facts, without divulging confidential conversations, so that they can support the family in prayer and practical ways. Use this time to educate the congregation about domestic violence, not only because everyone will be impacted by this situation, but also because other families are likely experiencing abuse in their homes as well.

• *Help to identify godly role models for her children and authentic spiritual direction for her.* The abusive pastor has represented a distorted view of God and misinterpreted Scripture, which may impact the entire family's ability to view God as loving and trustworthy. Helping them plug into a different faith community, even temporarily, will go a long way toward reaffirming the family's faith in God and the church.

The following practical steps are ways to provide assistance to all victims of family violence, but a pastor's family, because of their unique relationship to a congregation, may find their experience of leaving an abusive situation is more public. They particularly need the support of church members who will be their advocates in the faith community, including:

• Assurances that God does not expect her (or anyone) to endure abuse and oppression
• Help in making a safety plan that will move her and the children to a safe place
• Recommendations of a support group and encouragement to seek counseling
• Financial assistance so she can secure safe lodging and legal aid (order of protection, child support) if necessary
• Transportation to and from counseling sessions or court hearings to secure her safety

When the survivor and her children are in a safe place, the offending pastor must be relieved of his duties and referred to a treatment program for abusers. The couple should not resume living together, nor should he return to the pulpit until (and unless) real change and true repentance are evident. This transformation may take many months, and even years, so don't short-circuit the healing process by forcing a marital reconciliation or ministry restoration too soon.

Church leaders must determine how much financial support will be available to both parties, as well as devise a plan for the needs of the church body with an interim pastor until a longer-term decision about the church's leadership future can be made.

How to Help Him

If the pastor is reinstated following his treatment program, he needs to be held accountable to a selected group of godly men who cannot be swayed or easily manipulated and who are in constant contact with his wife to hear her side of the story.

If the pastor and his wife reconcile, extra vigilance must be taken to ensure her ongoing safety. One pastor's wife returned home after running errands. Trying to catch her off guard, her husband had parked his car several blocks away and was inside the house, waiting for her in the bedroom. He began demanding an account of her day, who she had spoken to, and where she had gone. After a time of badgering and threatening, he moved his car to the driveway, blocking her car so she could not leave. Although he had stopped physically battering his wife since attending the treatment program, his mind and heart were not transformed and she was still at risk. Members of the pastor's accountability group must never assume everything will be okay just because he has repented and attended counseling sessions.

Churches have the responsibility to call abusers to accountability. When the abuser is the pastor, there is an added responsibility to demonstrate to the outside world the compassion and grace of Christ, as well as to take a strong stand against oppression and abuse. Hiding evil or covering up a transgression to save the reputation of the church is not godly. By protecting the victims and providing for them in practical ways, the church shows the world it is a safe place where broken people can find refuge. Confronting an abuser, especially if he is the pastor, and standing by him as he faces a long road of confrontation, repentance, reciprocity toward those he has wronged (his family, the church family, and God), and accountability make a bold declaration that although God hates evil, God loves the evildoer.

The church represents Christ to a dying world. We can either be a weak, an ineffective, and a judgmental people who hide evil or kill our wounded or we can be the hands and feet of Jesus, offering justice to the oppressed and healing to the broken. The first scenario makes the world laugh at our hypocrisy and makes God weep, but the second scenario breathes life and hope into a world desperate to meet real people who have encountered a real God.

Isn't that the purpose of the church—to draw people to Christ? Our traditional definition of evangelism must encompass the whole of Christ's ministry—to preach good news to the poor, to heal the brokenhearted, to restore sight to the blind (spiritually as well as physically!), and to set the captives free (see Luke 4:18). Ministry that draws people to Christ needs to start at home, then move into our churches, then into our neighborhoods, and finally the world. Isn't that what Jesus taught?

Notes

1. Dee Engel, personal testimony, Yucaipa, CA. Used by permission.
2. Ibid.

CHAPTER 9

Counseling Dos and Don'ts

My job is to follow the Spirit's movement, never to try to move people on my own. I am to desire the Spirit's goal for my troubled friends, not a better marriage, but an aroused appetite for God that could lead to a better marriage. I am to wait for the Spirit to move and then tag along, to walk through doors he opens into their souls, not to insist they see something now and change.

—Dr. Larry Crabb, *Soul Talk*[1]

When a victim of family violence appears in your office frightened and confused, you may be the first person she has trusted with the deepest wounds of her soul. Responding in a way that makes her feel safe and understood is critical. She is not looking for a clever formula or a study in theology. She needs you to listen without judgment, to validate her experience, and to show compassion without pity. When she shares her most private thoughts, she needs to know you can be trusted to maintain confidentiality. Most pastors and counselors want to do the right thing; however, you can have all the right intentions yet cause great harm.

Common Counseling Mistakes

Listed below are some of the most common mistakes when dealing with domestic violence issues.

Missing Warning Signs

The smiling, confident woman sitting across from you may not see herself as an abused woman. She may complain about depression or express concern about her husband's anger—symptoms of a deeper wound. She may fiercely protect her husband's reputation out of a sense of duty, fear, or love.

Acknowledge her bravery and assure her she is not betraying her husband by seeking help. As you become more aware of the dynamics of domestic violence, you will be equipped to ask questions to determine her situation such as, "Do you ever feel frightened of him?" "What happens when you express an opinion different from his?" "How does he express his anger?" "Has he ever slapped or pushed you?" "Has he ever threatened you?" As her story unfolds, ask God to help you look beneath the surface and gently probe for truth she may be hesitant to reveal.

Disbelieving, Minimizing, or Incorrectly Defining Her Experience

A good counselor can validate and affirm a victim without agreeing with her or indicting the perpetrator by saying, "You are not alone. All abuse is wrong—no one deserves to be treated that way."

Don't assume that because physical violence has not occurred in the past, it won't happen in the future. One woman told her pastor about her husband's threat to kill her, but because neither the couple nor the husband had a history of physical violence, the pastor asked, "Did he hold a gun to your head?" and proceeded to lecture her about the sin of divorce.

Take verbal threats seriously (especially threats from the perpetrator to kill her and/or himself), and consider verbal abuse as destructive as physical violence. Don't assume the victim is safe just because she appears to be strong or brave.

Refusing to Believe the Abuser Could Do Such a Thing

Most abusers appear to be charming and devoted to their families; some claim to be committed to God. They can be master manipulators who often use Scripture to justify their use of power and control to keep their family in line. Some may present themselves as victims even though they are actually the perpetrator.

Pastors and counselors need to be aware that an abuser will blame others, attempt to confuse the pastor or counselor by distorting the facts, and try to manipulate and dominate the counseling session to divert the attention from his behavior to the faults of the victim.

Deciding Who Is Telling the Truth or Who Provoked Whom

The priority should always be to determine the level of safety and then act accordingly. The dynamics of domestic violence involve an imbalance of power and control, which requires a completely different response from most of the techniques used in marriage counseling. Suggesting behavioral changes for *both* partners would be ineffective and counterproductive because such a reciprocal expectation places implicit responsibility on the victim for the abuser's behavior. The perpetrator needs to work through issues of entitlement and superiority before his behavior will change for the long term.

Advising the Victim Not to Pursue Legal Safeguards

An abuser must be held accountable for his actions, even if it means embarrassment or time in jail. When evil is swept under the carpet, the message is loud and clear to the abuser that he can continue his behavior without any consequences. Do not advise a victim to drop a restraining order or not to press charges.

Some churches place an additional burden on the victim by requiring her to offer the abuser instant forgiveness and grace by going back home and refraining from pressing charges against him. However, the Scriptures clearly teach that even though God offers grace and forgiveness, God also requires true repentance and allows a person to experience the consequences of his sin.

Many times the only thing that will get through to an abuser is experiencing the reality of his actions and suffering the painful consequences. Pain may be the breakthrough to his denial and change; secrecy or a lack of consequences enables his behavior to continue.

Contacting the Perpetrator without the Victim's Permission

If you contact the perpetrator to tell him about his wife's visit without receiving her permission and without having a safety plan in place, the victim is in greater danger of physical harm. When the abuser realizes that his actions have been exposed and that his sense of power and control has been diminished, he may react with violence. Always have a safety plan in place for the victim and seek her permission before contacting the perpetrator.

Confronting the Perpetrator Alone

If you meet with the perpetrator, follow the Matthew 18 model and have a witness present at all meetings as a defense for potential lawsuits. Do not expect the perpetrator to admit his abusive behavior. He may suggest his wife is mentally unstable, blame her for pushing his buttons, or falsely claim she is violent toward him. If he does admit fault and appears to be repentant, proceed cautiously by requiring him to get counseling or to enroll in a long-term treatment program, not just an anger management class (see "Suggesting Anger Management Classes" below).

Counseling the Victim and the Perpetrator Together

Joint counseling of the victim and the abuser inhibits the victim's freedom to talk honestly about the situation. Joint counseling gives the abuser more power over the victim through intimidation and silent threats, which may not be apparent to the pastor or counselor. The victim may be in danger of retaliation following the counseling session.

Suggesting Anger Management Classes

Many abusers learn to divert their expressions of anger to appear in compliance with the anger management program. Changing an abuser has less to do with behavioral adjustments and more to do with attitude and heart adjustments. Anger management programs may be useful after the abuser has successfully completed a long-term treatment program, stopped all physical abuse, and demonstrated interest in pursuing a process of lifelong change.

Rescuing the Victim Rather Than Empowering Her

An abused woman wants to be safe and to have her opinions and choices respected. She needs affirmation, support, and encouragement—not more control. Rescuing her is another form of control and does not empower her to act out of her own strength to protect herself and her family.

One church offered temporary housing to a young female member and her child, but the leadership required her to submit to their control regarding her future. "If you pursue a divorce," they warned, "we will withdraw all our support." She had to choose between being homeless and adhering to their restrictions and ultimatums.

This church could have been her anchor in the storm—if they had offered her options that allowed her to choose the best path for herself and her family. She desperately needed to know her church would stand with her through the storm ahead—with financial support, counseling, advocacy, and childcare. With such support, she could pursue any necessary education or training and search for employment that would allow her to become independent. Instead, the church merely threw her a lifeline and then threatened to snatch it back later.

Making the Goal a Change in Behavior

Don't be satisfied with simply a change in the abuser's behavior, such as more frequent church attendance or less frequent outbursts of temper. You must dig deeper to find out what was driving the abusive behavior; otherwise, it will reappear again either in the same form or disguised as another abusive behavior. Recall Jesus' rebuke to the Pharisees who focused their behavior on external actions while their hearts were full of hypocrisy and lawlessness. He told them that to be clean on the outside they must first clean up the inside—heart and mind (Matthew 23:25-26).

Encouraging Reconciliation Too Soon

If the perpetrator has truly changed, he will be willing to wait as long as it takes to prove himself and rebuild trust. An apology, tears, promises, or a religious experience does not eliminate the need for maintaining safety for the victim until the change can be verified, over time, by professional counselors. A wise counselor knows the difference between remorse and true repentance. *Remorse* is being sorry for the consequences; *repentance* means turning around and walking in another direction. It is critical not to insist a woman reconcile with her abusive husband just because he has made a profession of faith or expressed remorse publicly. Just as family violence is predicated on a pattern of abusive behavior, so repentance must be evidenced by a pattern of transformed living—over time.

Holding the Victim Responsible for Keeping the Family Together

The breakup of the family should not be blamed on the victim for seeking safety but on the perpetrator who has violated the marriage covenant. Women should not be advised to stay in an abusive situation for the sake of the children. As noted earlier, although children benefit from being raised by both a mother and a father, experts believe a child suffers more negative long-term effects by staying in an abusive home.

Bill and Bethany's Story

Let's analyze the three scenarios presented in chapter 1 to identify why the counsel they received in the third scenario was wise and life affirming and why the counsel received in the first and second scenarios was shortsighted and potentially harmful.

In the first scenario, the pastor was more concerned in vindicating Bill than he was in believing Bethany. He did not offer his full attention or an open mind; therefore, she did not feel safe. His primary concern was insulating the church from being exposed to the messy situation (asking Bethany to resign her position) and protecting the so-called sanctity of the marriage at the expense of Bethany's welfare.

Is it wrong to protect the church and uphold marriage? Absolutely not. But neither institution should take priority over the life and safety of someone in peril. Jesus died on the cross to save lives, not institutions. When Bethany left the pastor's office, she felt as if her life had no value to God or to anyone else. The pastor was correct in suggesting additional counseling, but to suggest joint counseling was unwise and potentially dangerous to Bethany. He did not understand that this couple would not benefit from typical marriage counseling where two equals work together to overcome conflict or communication issues. His prayer for Bethany to do the right thing placed another burden on her shoulders, unfairly holding her responsible for the consequences of Bill's actions. This pastor lacked understanding of domestic violence and was too quick to act in his own wisdom instead of administering healing balm to a wounded soul.

In the second scenario, the counselor was more interested in fixing the problem (and taking great pride in his expertise) than he was in listening deeply and allowing God to use him as a life-giving connection between the water of life and Bethany's thirsty soul. His prescribed plan of action gave Bethany the message that if she worked harder God would heal the marriage. Once again, the focus is on Bethany's response rather than addressing the sin being committed against her. It's like telling a rape victim to change her style of clothing so the rapist will not be tempted—placing the blame and responsibility on her for his actions. The counselor's suggestion of the weekend retreat where the couple can reconnect is as if he asked Bethany to hug a whirling fan blade that will rip her to shreds. The counselor can be commended for his goal to salvage marriages, but that should be a secondary priority.

What Bethany really needs is to be heard and understood, to be cared for—and most of all, *to be safe.* After securing Bethany's physical safety, his priority as a counselor to Bethany as a survivor of family violence should be to engage in the battle going on in the depths of her soul—a need to connect with God, where she will find her deepest healing, satisfaction, and identity. Even healthy human relationships are not sufficient to heal her spirit, and religious rituals may leave her disillusioned and empty. Only a close encounter with Jesus will restore her joy, her peace, and her faith in God for a hope-filled future.

In the third scenario, Bethany finds sanctuary and hope. Let's examine the correct ways in which that pastoral counselor responded.

Correct Counseling Responses

After Bethany shared her story, the counselor assumed she was telling the truth and asked strategic questions to determine her level of safety. His support for her took the form of listening and understanding, validating her pain, determining her level of safety, offering options and waiting for her response, and taking immediate action.

Listening and Understanding

These are the keys to connecting with someone on a deeper level. Bethany's counselor asked probing questions that invited responses that not only helped him to understand her situation but allowed him to identify with her pain. Effective ministry begins with good listening skills and curiosity about the other person's journey. Instead of really listening, however, many people focus more on developing their response. In the book *Making Small Groups Work,* Drs. Henry Cloud and John Townsend write, "People do not listen to each other. Instead they preach, teach, advise, pontificate, and immediately talk about themselves. All those things might have their place at some point, but usually they are way down the list of priorities, way behind the need to just listen."[2]

Validating Her Pain

The healing process involves both grace and truth. Validating her pain is offering grace—administering healing to her wounds until she is strong enough to face the truth of her situation. By listening closely and identifying with Bethany's pain, the counselor was able to offer sincere words of affirmation and healing words of comfort. He didn't try to explain away Bill's abuse or to convince her that she was overreacting to the situation. Dr. Henry Cloud describes truth as the concrete wall of a gymnasium and grace as the foam pad attached to it to protect athletes when they crash up against the wall. Grace does not diminish or compromise the truth but protects us from being destroyed. In counseling a victim of abuse, it may be tempting to deny reality—for our own sake as well as for the victim, but grace creates a safe space to acknowledge the pain that often accompanies truth.

Determining Her Level of Safety

If the conversation is limited and the victim is not forthcoming, probe, look beneath, and ask questions (see page 77). Failing to do this is like prescribing Pepto-Bismol for a stomachache when the person needs immediate surgery to remove an infected appendix. As a doctor needs specialized training to make a proper diagnosis, pastors and counselors need training in the dynamics of domestic violence. Because training is either nonexistent or woefully inadequate in most seminaries and counseling programs, seeking help from experts in the field is crucial. You can read books on your own, attend seminars, or schedule workshops to train your church and staff. FOCUS Ministries, Inc. (focusministries1.org) is one organization that provides customized onsite training to pastors, churches, and organizations and sponsors training events for women interested in starting support groups for victims of domestic violence.

Offering Options and Waiting for Her Response

A wise pastor or counselor doesn't wait for a crisis to occur to start looking for resources to help victims of domestic violence. Along with becoming educated on the subject, knowing about community and nationwide resources available to the whole family is critical to responding quickly and effectively. Always present two or more options to the victim, then allow her to choose. Do not try to control or manipulate her into doing what you think is best. Even if she makes the wrong choice, in your opinion, your role is to provide support and safety when she is ready to accept it.

Keep in mind that in many women, Post Traumatic Stress Disorder may cause relational obstacles such as avoidance, emotional numbness, irritability, and hypervigilance. Understanding these symptoms will provide a critical insight for pastoral counselors who wonder why victims may resist relationships with others who offer safety, friendship, and support.

Taking Immediate Action

The first course of action is to offer her safety. Of the pastors Bethany contacted for help, one offered prayer but no practical resources; another said when God told him to move he would do something. Any hesitation to provide safety—whether due to lack of knowledge, fear of getting involved, or indecisiveness—may cost someone's life. Treatment programs and follow-up counseling are important but should take second priority to providing safety.

Strategic questions to ask a victim[3]

1. Describe what happens when the two of you argue or have a very bad fight.
2. Do you ever feel frightened of him?
3. What happens when you express an opinion different from his?
4. How does he speak to you when he is angry or frustrated?
5. Does he ever throw things or punch holes with his fist?
6. Has he ever slapped or hit you? Pushed you or blocked your exit from a room? Threatened you?
7. How does he react when you want to go out with friends or family?
8. Have you ever told anyone?
9. Are you concerned about your safety now?
10. Would you be willing to stay in a safe place tonight?

Wrong things to say to a victim:[4]

1. What did you do to provoke him?
2. Pray harder—prayer changes things.
3. Go home, cook your husband's favorite meal, and give him some extra attention.
4. The Bible says you need to forgive him seventy times seven.
5. Things could be worse.
6. If you try harder and become more submissive, your husband will change.
7. God hates divorce, so you must do whatever you can to hold your marriage together, even if it means suffering for Jesus.
8. Your children need a father, so it is up to you to keep the family together.
9. If he has not hit you before, you probably aren't in any danger now.

10. He is a good man and a good provider. He may be under a lot of stress at work. Maybe you need to be more understanding and provide a peaceful refuge at home.

A woman is in imminent danger if . . .[5]

- He has threatened her life. Take it seriously!
- He has battered her recently or if she sustained injuries each time he battered her in the past.
- He has weapons in the home or has recently bought a gun.
- He has locked her in the house or restricted her freedom.
- He has killed or injured her pet.
- He talks about dreams involving murder (either his or hers).
- He has threatened to hurt or kill himself, the children, and her if she leaves.

Statements to confront the perpetrator[6]

1. I am here to support you and help your family, but I do not condone hitting your wife or treating her with disrespect.
2. I will not desert you, but I will not excuse your behavior either.
3. As long as you continue to be violent, I will not provide or recommend joint counseling.
4. By not stopping the abuse, you may go to jail or lose your family. I will encourage your wife to call the police the next time you hit her or terrorize her.
5. If you want help, I will help you find a long-term group treatment program where you will learn to value your wife's freedom and worth as a person more than your need to control. I will encourage you to join an accountability group or a recovery group where you can share your struggles with others who care about you.
6. I will hold you accountable by checking with your wife often to see how things are going.
7. If your wife feels unsafe, I will help her find a safe place to stay.
8. Your role as head of the home is to be a servant leader, not to control and dominate. Scripture does not give you the right to punish your wife or disrespect her in any way.

Structured Separations

Many pastors and marriage counselors recommend a couple stay together when they are working out conflicts in their marriage. When dealing with domestic violence, however, this is not a wise approach. When safety is an issue due to physical violence or verbal and emotional abuse is severe, a structured separation is usually a better solution. Dr. Henry Cloud gives the following advice: "The greater the chaos, the greater the structure that is needed. If you get hit by a car, you don't need a band-aid from Rite-Aid. You need a very structured environment that is germ-free (nobody there to hurt you, no new toxins) where experts will help you heal."[7]

The goal for a structured separation is for each person to work diligently with a support group, counselor, treatment program, or recovery group on specific issues. The separation will give them time to heal and grow, to discover the real issues in the breakdown of the relationship, and to make lasting changes in behavior and attitude. A good separation will have a structure with specific goals and tasks for each person, rules by which both people abide, and a timetable to evaluate their progress. The goals, rules, and structure are different for each relationship and need to be developed and followed with flexibility and grace.

When trust is rebuilt and safety is no longer an issue, then reconciliation can be a goal. At a minimum, a six-to-twelve-month separation is recommended if physical abuse or addictions are among the problems being addressed. In some cases, reconciliation may not be possible.

Sample structured separation

1. Decide where each party will live and how communication will take place. If safety is an issue, the victim should file for an order of protection or make sure meetings are held in a public place with a third party present.
2. If children are involved, agree on a visitation schedule. If violence is an issue, the couple should meet in a public place to drop off or pick up the children.
3. Agree on financial issues such as who will pay the bills and provide child support. If an agreement cannot be reached

between the couple, seek the help of a mediator or attorney.
4. Schedule time intervals for evaluation of the situation.
5. Verbal, emotional, or physical abuse; harassment; or stalking will not be tolerated by either person.
6. Each person will take responsibility for his or her next steps in response to the abusive realtionship. (For the victim, this often involves wrestling with character traits such as passivity or a lack of healthy boundaries.) Victims will attend a support group or receive individual counseling. Perpetrators will attend a long-term treatment program or commit to individual counseling.

Additional resources may be found in Appendix A to help victims (crisis flow chart, safety plan, checklist of needs, etc.) and in Appendix B to help perpetrators (checklist to identify abusive characteristics, signs he has changed, and treatment programs).

You as a pastor or a counselor are one of the "first responders" to victims of domestic violence and serve a vital role in helping the victim, the abuser, and their family move toward healing. The next chapter explores how churches can also serve and assist the victims and perpetrators of domestic violence.

Notes

1. Larry Crabb, *Soul Talk* (Nashville: Integrity Publishers, 2003), 241.
2. Henry Cloud and John Townsend, *Making Small Groups Work* (Grand Rapids: Zondervan, 2003), 202–03.
3. "Dos and Don'ts of Counseling," *Pastor's Guide—Dealing with Domestic Violence* (Elmhurst, IL: FOCUS Ministries, Inc., 2005), n.p. Used by permission.
4. Ibid.
5. Ibid.
6. Ibid.
7. "Trauma and Abuse: Too Much Hurt to Handle," audio recording, Monday Night Solutions for Life, Cloud-Townsend Resources. Order at http://cloudtownsendstore.com.

CHAPTER 10

The Church's Role and Response

As postmodernism continues its valueless sweep across America, abuse of all types will increase when self-centered egos collide. Is the church in America up to facing its new reality? Are we church leaders willing to accept the risks, including death threats against us, as we reach out to defend those who cannot defend themselves?

—Steve Dresselhaus, TEAM missionary pastor, La Paz, Mexico[1]

Family violence is a crime that destroys families. Yet this crime is often ignored or swept under the carpet in churches. Many American churches have taken a bold stand against abortion, gambling, pornography, adultery, homosexuality, cohabitation by singles, and other issues. Have our churches become forums for morality and sterile worship instead of care centers of spiritual healing where broken people can find hope? Perhaps in addition to the crime of assault in violent homes, we in the church have committed a greater crime against God by ignoring the pain and suffering of the oppressed.

Why Churches Ignore Abuse

The most common reasons domestic violence is not addressed in many churches include concerns about divorce, not wanting to interfere in family business, fear of the risks, lack of knowledge, apathy, fear of exposing the pastor's abuse, other ministry priorities, and concern for appearances.

Divorce

Some pastors feel that discussing abuse and encouraging victims to speak out and seek help would cause an increase in divorces. However, most women in abusive situations are not initially seeking a divorce—they just want the disrespect and violence to stop. For most, divorce is the last resort when the abuser refuses to change. The safety of women and children should never be sacrificed on the altar of the institution of marriage. A wise pastor once said, "It is possible for a divorced woman to be reconciled to her husband, but reconciliation will never be possible if she is dead!"

Family Business

By keeping family secrets and putting on good-little-church-people masks that make us appear to be godly, our families and churches have become dysfunctional. The unspoken rule is, "Don't discuss family business at church." However, what happens in the family always impacts the church family. Paul wrote, "If one member suffers, all the members suffer . . ." (1 Corinthians 12:26, NKJV). What correlation might there be between anemic churches and the state of the unions in their midst?

Fear of the Risks

Getting involved in the lives of broken people is always messy, time-consuming, and risky—especially when domestic violence is part of the dynamic. An angry abuser may threaten to sue the pastor and church for interfering in his family's business by helping his wife and children. In the most extreme case, the abuser may show up during a church service with a weapon, and people may be injured or killed. Pastors may receive personal death threats or implied threats against their family members or congregation. These risks cause some pastors and churches to turn a blind eye to the problem so that they can maintain comfort and safety for themselves and their congregations. How this must sadden the heart of God, who loves justice and hears the cry of the oppressed

(Psalm 34:15-18). God's primary mission for the church was not to institute programs for believers inside the walls of a safe, comfortable building. God called us to go out into the world and get involved in the lives of people—to serve others (1 Peter 4:10), to take care of the widows and orphans (James 1:27), and to be willing to lose our lives for his sake (Matthew 10:39).

Lack of Knowledge

Understanding the dynamics of domestic violence is crucial to helping both the victim and the perpetrator. If a pastor feels adequately equipped to deal with domestic violence using marriage-counseling techniques, that pastor is tragically misguided and does not understand the serious nature of abuse. Read Hosea 4 to see how God responds to spiritual leaders whose refusal of knowledge brought destruction to God's people. Pastors must first acknowledge a problem exists, then educate and equip themselves to deal with the problem, and then raise awareness in their congregation.

Apathy

Many Christians have become mere observers of social injustice and sin instead of becoming salt and light to a dying world. When our churches are unresponsive or indifferent to domestic violence, we are as guilty as the priest and Levite who walked past the wounded man in the story of the good Samaritan in Luke 10. By failing to be like Jesus and obey his command to "Go and do likewise" (Luke 10:37, NKJV), we are inviting God's judgment (Revelation 3:16-17).

Exposing the Pastor's Abuse

Sadly, some abusers are cleverly disguised as shepherds of the flock. In our work with victims of domestic violence, we have received an overwhelming response from pastors' wives who report being verbally and physically abused at home while their husbands are perceived as loving, powerful ministers of the gospel. When power and control are rooted in a pastor's heart, as they are in abusive relationships, a discussion of domestic violence in church might lead to truth telling and exposure of his abuse at home.

A Low Ministry Priority

Many churches make evangelism their main priority and may not feel that saving lives is as important as saving souls. However, according to the example set by Jesus, evangelism and love in action are two sides of the same coin. The good news is not only for those who need forgiveness of sins but also for the poor, the captives, the blind, and the oppressed (Luke 4:18). Those who are oppressed by domestic violence need the gospel! Perhaps the church needs to reflect Jesus' style of evangelism— showing kindness and meeting needs as the first step to turning hearts toward God.

Appearances

Many congregations take pride in representing themselves as good, moral people who have solid marriages and healthy families. But according to statistics, one in every four women in each church community is experiencing domestic violence or has at some point in the past. As congregation members, we need to take off the masks of perfection and allow the world to see that we are broken people in need of a Savior. Jesus didn't come to save righteous people—he came to save sinners (Matthew 9:12-13). As musician Todd Agnew says, "We don't need to show the world how good we are so they will want to be with us. They need to understand that we're broken, and that broken people can come and be whole."[2]

Called to Minister

The call of each church community is to minister to those who are hurting, broken, and oppressed. God indicted the religious community of Ezekiel's day with the words, "You have not strengthened the weak or healed the sick or bound up the injured. You have not brought back the strays or searched for the lost. You have ruled them harshly and brutally" (Ezekiel 34:4, NIV).

Jesus warned the religious leaders of his day: "How terrible it will be for you teachers of religious law and you Pharisees. Hypocrites! For you are careful to tithe even the tiniest part of your income, but you ignore the important things of the law—justice, mercy, and faith" (Matthew 23:23, NLT).

The following statements, representing the experiences of women throughout the United States who turned to their church for help, will both challenge and encourage you.

Ways My Church Was Not Helpful

- Many people found it difficult to believe me.
- I felt like the church abandoned me.
- I was shunned by almost all the leaders. I needed a safe place when I was enduring the abuse, yet going to church only opened me up for more abuse from the church.
- I wish they had heard my cries when I went to the altar feeling like I was tremendously dirty and filthy.
- People kept telling me, "God hates divorce," and quoting Scripture passages. They saw my decision to leave as abandonment. They shunned me and treated me as if I were the perpetrator.
- The place where I used to receive peace and solace became a battleground.
- Many people did not ask what they could do to help. I had a hard time asking for help.
- They fell for his charm and he began to play them—going to church all the time, making friends with those who would listen. They wrote letters of recommendation to the court praising his service and dedication to the Lord. Even when he was reported to child protective services, the church stood by him saying he would never hurt his children.
- They asked, "How could you let this happen to you?" They told me, "It's over—forget it."
- They said, "Hang in there and trust the Lord to deliver you. Just pray about it."
- They asked me to give up teaching Sunday school.
- They required me to keep quiet about my situation in public and asked me not to make prayer requests at church unless it was for health issues.
- They refused to help me unless I agreed not to pursue a divorce.

Ways My Church Was Helpful

- They welcomed me with open arms, never judged, just loved and accepted me. It was as if Jesus himself wrapped his arms around me.
- They did not allow my husband to attend the same service as me, and when he showed up the men escorted him outside.
- They helped with child care, car repairs, and household needs.
- They connected me with a godly mentor who stuck with me like glue in a gentle, loving way, allowing me to go at my own pace.
- Two deacons escorted me to every court or counseling appointment where my husband would be present.
- They provided funds for a professional counselor and offered free help with financial planning.
- Various families invited my children and me to join them for recreational outings, birthday celebrations, meals at a restaurant, etc.
- One family allowed us to stay in their home until we could make it on our own.
- They helped us find a place to live and paid the first month's rent. They helped me find a job so I could support myself and my children.
- They remembered us on holidays and birthdays.
- They listened, they prayed, and they loved us.

Steve Dresselhaus is a missionary pastor serving in La Paz, Mexico, with the mission agency TEAM. He has bravely led his church to take a stand against domestic violence. They have ministered to many women and children by providing safe houses, emergency shelter, and practical necessities for daily living. Steve and other church leaders have been subjected to death threats and machete attacks from violent abusers who seek to harm them for helping the abusers' wives and children. Steve writes:

A call comes from the Mexican government's office of Integral Development of the Family. "We have a woman and two children here with us. The woman's husband, a police officer, previously threatened her with his service revolver, holding it against her head and later against her belly and unborn child. Just now he tried to run over her with his car. Can you hide her? We have no place to take her."

The question, needing an immediate answer, is the now ubiquitous but just as often ignored "WWJD?" What *would* Jesus do in this instance? Would he have said to this woman, "Be fed and clothed, and may his bullets never reach you?" Or would our Lord have said, "Come to me, you who are weary and heavy laden, and I will give you rest?" Is there any doubt what Jesus would do? . . . Are we church leaders willing to accept the risks, including death threats against us, as we reach out to defend those who cannot defend themselves? . . . Now it is time to transform . . . our world by "letting our light so shine before men that they may see our good works and glorify our Father which is in heaven."[3]

In writing this book, our prayer is that every pastor reading it will accept Steve's challenge to represent Jesus to those who cannot defend themselves. The compassion and heart for hurting people in the churches with whom we have consulted encourages us. Three in particular have begun the process of reaching out to families involved in domestic violence and serve as role models for other churches, regardless of size: the Moody Church in Chicago, Illinois; Coral Ridge Presbyterian Church in Ft. Lauderdale, Florida; and Providence Baptist Church in Raleigh, North Carolina.

What Churches Can Do

If your church wants to begin an effective ministry to families suffering in domestic violence, begin by setting up a task force of men and women who have a heart for ministry to hurting people. This group may include a survivor of domestic violence, a lay or professional counselor with expertise in this area, a social worker, a pastoral care leader, and a volunteer at a local shelter, and the like. The task force may consider scheduling a consultation or seminar with FOCUS Ministries or a similar organization to help develop a strategic plan customized to your church's needs.

The task force duties may include the following:

- Setting a timeline for completing the plan
- Scheduling regular meetings
- Researching the need in your church and surrounding areas
- Developing a list of resources available through secular and faith-based agencies

In addition, the task force needs to answer questions about how your church will handle safety and liability, what you will do if an abuser attends the same service as the victim, what resources are available within and outside your church, what assistance you will provide to victims and their children, and how you will deal with abusers who are church members.

Four main areas in the strategic plan need to be developed: education, awareness, advocacy, and support.

Education

Training pastors, counselors, and church leaders about the dynamics of domestic violence is essential. Start by scheduling, at a minimum, a half-day seminar for pastors and counselors,[4] and provide subsequent workshops for women's ministry leaders, women mentors, youth and children's ministry leaders, and Sunday school teachers. Provide continuing education annually for each of these groups, and encourage them to read books and articles about domestic violence periodically.

Awareness

The pastor has a great opportunity to raise the awareness and educate the congregation by preaching a series of sermons on domestic violence. Plan to do this at least annually, perhaps during October, which is Domestic Violence Awareness month. An excellent sermon on domestic violence called "A Destructive Secret" by Pastor Erwin Lutzer is available as part of an audiotape series called "Reclaiming the Family" (see http://moodychurch.org). Testimonies by survivors of domestic violence are another powerful way to help a congregation understand what living in an abusive home is like. In women's restrooms and areas where women congregate, display information about where to get help, such as hotline phone numbers and a list of agencies, support groups and shelters, and brochures on abuse. Purchase books on domestic violence for the church library. Don't miss opportunities during marriage seminars and men's and women's conferences and retreats to include a workshop and resources (books and free literature) on the subject of domestic violence.

Advocacy

Begin by appointing a contact person in your church, one person who can respond to needs as they arise. Develop a crisis flowchart to direct victims quickly and wisely to the right options. (See Appendix A for an example.) Also organize a support team to which the contact person can turn for help.

Consider purchasing a cell phone that can be shared among the support team members and used as a hotline number, because it cannot be traced to a person's home address. If the church has voice mail, set up a separate mailbox for crisis calls and have a member of the support team check it frequently.

The church's website is also a great way to provide information for victims online. Provide a link to a separate e-mail address at the church that one person from the support team would check and respond to.

A referral list of agencies, counselors, attorneys, shelters, and support groups will be invaluable when someone comes to you for help. Make sure each pastor and counselor has a copy of this list as well. The contact person/advocate should also become familiar with the local court system and state laws so he or she can help the victim understand her options.

Support

Because safety is the priority, a personal safety plan needs to be developed for victims and a safety plan should be put in place for the church. A free eight-page safety plan is available for download at http://www.focusministries1.org, and a sample safety plan for the church is included in the *Pastor's Guide—Dealing with Domestic Violence*, which can be ordered online.

Next, establish guidelines for how the church will meet practical needs such as housing, food, transportation, clothing, and so

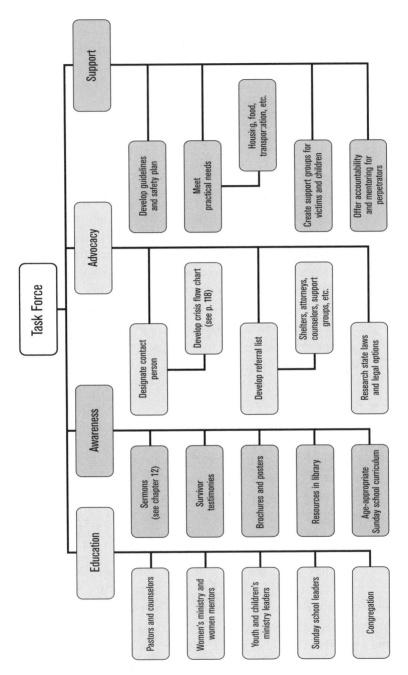

Figure 10.1 Task Force Strategic Plan

Copyright © 2006 by FOCUS Ministries. Used by permission.

forth. Your church can partner with local agencies to share the financial burden and to provide long-term care for the family in crisis. Your church may also choose to start support groups for the victim and children or a treatment program/accountability group for the abuser. Relational support is critical to the safety and growth of the family in crisis. Giving money and providing resources is not enough. The family needs the body of Christ to walk alongside them, encouraging and mentoring them as they heal and grow.

Putting It Together

A good way to develop your strategic plan is to have task force members write down each idea or goal on a 3″ x 5″ card. Arrange the cards randomly under the four main headings (education, awareness, advocacy, support) and prioritize each section according to urgency of the need and feasibility to accomplish the goal. Then develop a flow chart similar to the one illustrated on page 90.

Don't wait until you have all the pieces to the puzzle in place before you take action to help victims. Use the resources you have and rely on outside agencies to supplement what you don't yet have in place. Instead of being overwhelmed by the enormous needs around you and doing nothing, ask God to help you meet the needs of the next person you observe who needs help. Pray for the ability to see broken and hurting people through God's eyes and to respond to them with the compassion of Jesus.

Provide financial support for the work of your local domestic violence agencies and national faith-based organizations. To keep your church informed, invite their representatives to speak about their work during a church service or missions conference. For example, Harvard Avenue Evangelical Free Church in Villa Park, Illinois, one of our supporting churches, considers us missionaries who offer hope to women who are hurting. The church has responded to the needs around them by mobilizing a work team to help repair our Women's Center in Madisonville, Kentucky, and by providing monthly support through its missions budget.

Regardless of a church's size, there is something each one can do. We must not close our eyes and ears to the cries of those who are hurting, when we have resources and hope to share with them and a mandate from God to get involved:

Rescue those who are unjustly sentenced to death; don't stand back and let them die. Don't try to avoid responsibility by saying you didn't know about it. For God knows all hearts, and he sees you. He keeps watch over your soul, and *he knows you knew!* And he will judge all people according to what they have done. (Proverbs 24:11-12, NLT; italics added)

Notes

1. "What the Church Can Do," *Pastor's Guide—Dealing with Domestic Violence* (Elmhurst, IL: FOCUS Ministries, Inc., 2005), n.p.
2. Todd Agnew, during live concert, Pataskala, OH (June 25, 2006) (www.Todd Agnew.com). Ardent Records (www.ardentrecords.com), VanLiere-Wilcox Management (vanlierewilcox.com). Used by permission.
3. Steve Dresselhaus, "A Pastor's Challenge," in *Pastor's Guide—Dealing with Domestic Violence,* section 9 (Elmhurst, IL: FOCUS Ministries, Inc., 2005), n.p.
4. For seminars and materials, see "Domestic Violence Organizations and Ministries" in Appendix A, pages 128–36.

CHAPTER 11

Spiritual Direction

> If *all* you do is help women deal with domestic violence, you have done them a great disservice! If your primary goal is to help them find safety from an abusive husband, you are fighting the wrong battle. When you are more devoted to saving a marriage or raising good children than you are [interested] in pursuing God, you are putting second things first.
>
> —*Train the Trainer,* FOCUS Ministries, Inc.[1]

God has been faithful to equip people with knowledge, experience, and insight that help all of us minister to survivors of family violence. Pastors, counselors, and lay leaders have a responsibility to use every tool at their disposal to lead victims into a safe space where physical, emotional, psychological, and financial restoration can begin. However, addressing the immediate crisis is not enough. Efforts over the long term need to go beyond physical safety and economic stability to discern the deeper issues that led the victim into that place of vulnerability—and the invisible wounds the abuse inflicted on her vulnerable spirit. The body of Christ has a responsibility to equip her with the spiritual direction she needs to find hope and help in God, long after the pastoral or clinical counseling sessions have ended.

After physical safety is established for the victim, the goals should be to foster an inner healing in her spirit and to provoke within her a desire to encounter God. The healing process begins by digging beneath the surface of the problem to the struggle going on deep within her heart and soul, a struggle that in many individuals long predates the current experience of family violence. Uncovering that deeper wound is painful—and as vital as performing surgery to remove a cancerous tumor instead of merely treating its symptoms with two aspirin and a Band-Aid.

Spiritual Direction for Victims

The person who has suffered at the hands of an abuser, particularly over any length of time, may have been wounded before the current abusive relationship began. Therefore the latest experience with abuse will spark, or feed the smoldering flames of, the victim's negative views of self, of the opposite sex in general, and even of God. Look beneath the surface of a woman who has been battered (verbally, emotionally, or physically) and you will find a wounded daughter of Eve whose perception of the world and its Creator may be painfully distorted. She may express those views with anger, despair, confusion, or doubt. Consider just a few of the beliefs other survivors have confessed:

> "I feel like God was holding out on me. I prayed for a godly husband—and now look at me!"
>
> "How can I believe God is good when he allowed so many bad things to happen to me?"
>
> "I know the Bible says God is all powerful, so why didn't God use that power to protect me?"
>
> "I feel like God let me down. The only one I trust to do what's best for me is me."
>
> "I guess I'm not a good person. God was punishing me for my sins by letting my husband hit me."
>
> "I can't leave him. My pastor says God hates divorce, and I can't afford to have God hate me too."

Do you discern the conflicting responses in the hearts of these victims? Some blame themselves, assuming that the abuse is deserved—God's judgment on their own sins. Others blame God, unable to understand how a good God could allow such pain in the lives of God's children. Some are just plain confused—desperately trying to make sense of their traumatic experience in light of the faith to which they continue to cling.

A victim of domestic violence has a lot more issues to deal with than the abuse itself. She struggles with internal doubt and guilt as well as external expectations and pressures of others. Some of the issues with which a victim struggles include the following:

- The blinders of pain and suffering
- The problem of evil
- Low self-esteem
- Unhealthy boundaries
- God-in-a-bottle
- Fear
- The illusion of self-sufficiency
- The need for love

The Blinders of Pain and Suffering

Many have been so traumatized, bruised, battered, and betrayed they are barely surviving one day at a time. Pain and suffering have a tendency to focus a victim's gaze on the immediate circumstances—the basic needs of life and the necessity of pushing beyond the past to survive the present. They attempt to hold down full-time jobs, raise children, and maintain a household but often need help in lifting their eyes from the details of life to look to God, who can help them work through their circumstances.

The Problem of Evil

"Why do bad things happen to good people?" is an age-old question, and women looking for divine justice in the face of family violence wonder that and more: Why does God allow evil? Why doesn't God intervene to spare me and my children? Is God really there? Does God care? Pastors and counselors may not be able to answer definitively the problem of evil itself, but they can steadfastly point survivors toward a good God. To a spirit all but deafened by the din of verbal abuse and physical violence, the voice of God can offer a whisper of hope in the face of Job-like suffering.

Low Self-Esteem

The issue of low self-esteem is both a cause and an effect of family violence. A person with low self-esteem is often willing to accept criticism and abuse because she believes she deserves it or because she doesn't believe that she can expect anything better from life or relationships. Abuse only reinforces existing feelings of inferiority and unworthiness. Pastors and counselors can intervene in this issue by communicating scriptural principles relating to our creation in God's image (see Genesis 1:27), God's delight in us as his beloved (Zephaniah 3:17), and biblical principles relating to the good and hopeful future God has in mind for each of us (see Jeremiah 29:11). When women replace the abusive messages of contempt and disrespect with the message of Jesus' love and desire to know them intimately, their value and reason for living will be restored.

Unhealthy Boundaries

Too many women are people pleasers who have depended on their husbands to give them an identity. That reliance on anyone else to define a person's identity is dangerous even in a respectful marriage partnership and toxic in a relationship that is abusive. Therapists describe such relationships as *codependent*—where one participant is controlled or manipulated by a perceived need for the other, who is himself addicted to a substance or a behavior. In an abusive marriage, the victim is most often addicted to a spouse who is addicted to alcohol, rage, or simply a desire for control. The counselor of such a victim can encourage her to establish new personal boundaries that are oriented with God at the center. The person who finds her identity in the Lord is much better positioned to discover the road to healing—and not more hurt.

God-in-a-Bottle

It is a mistake to think of God as a genie in a bottle—that if you close your eyes, rub your cross jewelry, and pray real hard, the Lord will grant your wish. The "name it and claim it" theology that has become increasingly popular in the church today has many problems. One of them is that when God does not meet people's expectations, they feel betrayed by the church, the faith, or even God. Individuals who have embraced this theology have a particular challenge trying to reconcile their understanding of God with an experience of family violence or any personal trauma. Discovering in such a painful way that God is not a genie in a bottle who grants prayerful wishes or a vending-machine deity who dispenses treats if the coins of good works are inserted is devastating. The pastoral counselor will have some serious work in helping this person dismantle a distorted image of God before she can come again to a simple trust in the Lord's ability to work good, even through painful circumstances.

Fear

This issue encompasses the natural fear of taking a stand against the abuser—the physical risks of retaliation and retribution by the abuser himself and the financial risks of leaving home and even job or community—as well as the fear of reaction from family, mutual friends of the couple, and fellow believers in the church. Some victims fear God's judgment, whether for lacking faith or failing as a good enough spouse and parent. Counselors need to reassure these survivors that God loves them and demands justice on their behalf. If such a God is for them, no abuser, no judgmental church member, and no self-righteous friend can stand against them. If the victim struggles with a sense of guilt and responsibility, the pastoral counselor may have the privilege of offering God's forgiveness and grace instead of the condemnation the survivor fears.

The Illusion of Self-Sufficiency

After experiencing the acute vulnerability and helplessness of family violence, many survivors react with a sometimes defiant and often desperate need for control and self-sufficiency. Feeling betrayed by intimate friends and family who could not or would not help, experiencing judgment or avoidance from the church, recognizing the limitations of the criminal justice system—these all reinforce a sense that no one can be trusted. Wanting never to be at the mercy of another person, the victim resolves to stand alone. Never trust a man again. Never trust a church again. Never trust the police or courts again. Maybe even never trust God again. Of course, no one survives for long in isolation; no one can ever be truly self-sufficient. From the beginning of time, God recognized that it isn't good for a human being to be alone. After all, we are created in God's own image, and God exists in eternal fellowship within the Trinity. The counselor who works with a survivor striving for self-sufficiency would be wise to offer gentle but consistent counsel on rebuilding trust and establishing new and, as appropriate, renewed connections with family and friends.

The Need for Love

Women often seek fulfillment in life from a human relationship instead of allowing God to fill them up first. They try to quench their thirst for love with water from broken cisterns (Jeremiah 2:13) and pursue serial or promiscuous relationships—often involving high-risk sexual involvements—instead of seeking the living water Jesus offers, the unconditional and faithful love that will satisfy. Musician Todd Agnew has described our tendency to look to God solely as the bread *giver*, instead of looking to the Lord as the Bread of Life that will fill us up. When women allow God to fill them up with divine love, the resulting intimacy and peace let other people off the hook for not being able to satisfy the craving that only God can fill.

Many survivors of violence struggle with learning to trust again—to trust men specifically, to trust people in general, and even to trust God. That struggle has profound spiritual dimensions in addition to its practical effects, which are not difficult to understand. After all, most survivors of family violence experienced the abuse at the hands of someone very close to them, someone they knew and cared about intimately, someone whom they probably believed God had placed in their lives. Abuse is a violation of trust, a betrayal of the covenant relationship. Is it any wonder that survivors often experience distrust in relationships—including a terrifying distrust that God is still good, still in control, and still has her best interests at heart?

Such survivors need someone to walk alongside them as they face these issues—someone who will understand the struggle and the reasons behind it and will gently exhort the survivor to take the risks inherent in learning to trust and to love again. An encounter with the God who has the power to transform her life and redeem the past is probably the most critical step in that process. A pastor or counselor can encourage the survivor to dig into the Scriptures and allow God to reveal himself to her. This encounter is not the same as attending a weekly Bible study or having a daily devotional time. Rather, it is a personal pursuit of the Living Word—the God who is present, active, and encountered in the Scriptures. The study of Jesus' life as described in the Gospels can be a transforming experience. It can transform her image of God and gradually transform her image of herself as well.

If you are a pastor or counselor be ready to suggest the Scriptures recommended in this book and any others you may have discovered in your own faith journey. Be prepared to talk through the survivor's doubts, fears, and uncertainties with patience and empathy. A fresh reading of the Gospels would also benefit you as counselor and guide. The best way to help a person experience transformation in Jesus is to reflect Christ's love in your own words and deeds.

Spiritual Direction for Abusers

To understand the heart of an abuser, we can look at the first violent man—Cain. According to Genesis 4:1-16, Cain was the first baby born into this world. As an adult, he became guilty of the first murder—and it wasn't just a regular homicide. He committed the first fratricide—by killing his own brother. Cain couldn't blame his violence on the baggage of generations of dysfunctional family history. His parents, Adam and Eve, weren't perfect. In fact, the Bible says that sin entered the world through them. Still, Cain had been taught the same principles of life as his righteous brother, Abel, but it was Cain who allowed the roots of sin to twist their way into his heart and mind, distorting his thinking and hardening his heart to the point that he was willing to murder.

Ecclesiastes 1:9 observes that there is nothing new under the sun, so perhaps a study of the biblical record about Cain's character will give us some insight into the heart and mind of abusers today. What is it that makes a man become an abuser? Consider the following characteristics:

- He is right in his own eyes.
- He is jealous and envious.
- He has "good enough" religion.
- He is arrogant and narcissistic.
- He is angry.
- He lies and avoids responsibility.
- He is self-absorbed and lacks remorse.
- He refuses advice.

He Is Right in His Own Eyes

Cain was offended because God accepted Abel's sacrifice but rejected Cain's own. God responded to that resentment by urging Cain, "If you do well, will you not be accepted?" (Genesis 4:7, ESV). Cain didn't answer the Lord. Apparently he wasn't interested in being corrected; he wasn't interested in hearing about doing the right thing. It seems that he already felt righteous—in his own eyes. He wanted life on his own terms, instead of submitting to God who has all the answers. When an abuser feels justified in his behavior or self-righteous in his actions, the challenging task of the pastor or counselor is to discern this foolish spirit (see Proverbs 12:15) and invite the abuser to repent and do the right thing—in God's eyes.

He Is Jealous and Envious

Scripture doesn't mention the relationship between Cain and Abel prior to adulthood, when they both brought an offering to God, but perhaps Cain, as the elder brother, was often competing for his parents' attention and approval after Abel was born. What is certain, however, is that when God showed regard for Abel's sacrifice and none for Cain's, Cain reacted with a surge of resentment and jealousy—emotions that turned deadly, even when the Lord intervened to offer Cain a chance to redeem himself. An abuser's violence may be similarly motivated by jealousy or envy—and like

Cain, an abuser may direct that violent emotion toward whomever he holds responsible for the disrespect or loss of face he experiences. Pastors and counselors would be wise to seek the root of such jealous resentment and help the abuser replace old messages of inferiority with the truth from Scripture (see Psalm 139).

He Has "Good Enough" Religion

Cain settled for *doing* religious acts of service rather than *being* a godly man. He brought a sacrifice before the Lord and thought that was sufficient to earn God's approval. We don't know why God disregarded Cain's offering; scholars have a variety of theories, ranging from the type of offering (not a blood sacrifice) to the quality of the offering (not the first fruits) to the attitude with which it was offered. All we know from the story, however, is that when Cain failed to impress God with his sacrifice, he seemed to reject any desire to please God with his actions. Abusers inside the church often pride themselves on obeying the letter of the law—in tithing, acts of service, ministry commitments, or regular church attendance—but they fail to understand how their violence (verbal, emotional, sexual, or physical) violates the spirit of one of the greatest commandments—to love one another (Matthew 22:37-40). A pastoral counselor has the opportunity to clarify God's desire for obedience over sacrifice and for the laws of love over rigid adherence to the other laws.

He Is Arrogant and Narcissistic

Perhaps part of Cain's envy and jealousy came from a need to be the center of attention, a privilege he lost when his brother was born. Cain clearly had a sense of entitlement—believing that God *should* have approved of his sacrifice—and that suggests a spirit of arrogance as well. Counselors who work with abusers should be watchful for an attitude of entitlement or a need to be the center of attention. Egocentric tendencies are often rooted in a spirit of arrogance or narcissism. When an abuser goes through life assuming it is all about him—his desires, his rights, his feelings, his stuff—he lacks sensitivity to the feelings, desires, rights, or property of others. The counselor's role is to challenge such ego-centrism and remind the abuser of the biblical mandate to imitate Christ's humility and spirit of service (see Philippians 2:1-11) .

He Is Angry

Anger is a critical facet of Cain's character. He was angry with God and directed it toward his brother, who was a much closer and an easier target. It seems likely that the anger didn't originate only in this particular instance. Violence often emerges from anger that simmers deep within the heart of a person. The fact that Cain's anger was misdirected suggests that he wasn't just a man who got angry one day but an angry man who acted on it one day. For many abusers, simmering anger boils into rage that ultimately consumes them (Proverbs 29:11). Pastoral counselors who become aware of such rage in an abuser should be prayerful and cautious when navigating the issues that trigger it.

He Lies and Avoids Responsibility

When God asked Cain, "Where is your brother?" Cain diverted the attention from his actions by saying, "Am I my brother's keeper?" The implication was a lie—suggesting that he didn't know his brother's whereabouts and that he shouldn't be responsible for knowing. Abusers take a variety of approaches to these strategies. Some will lie and accuse their victims of being the perpetrator. Others will make excuses for themselves by claiming they were under stress or temporarily deranged because of extenuating circumstances. The church and the courts often become complicit in such attempts by the abuser to lie or to avoid responsibility by allowing themselves to be deceived ("It's never happened before") or persuaded ("It won't ever happen again").

God offers a very different model for responding to family violence. Genesis 4:10 says that God heard the cry of Abel's blood—and the Lord confronted Cain, holding him responsible for his actions. Let us stop sweeping abuse under the carpet of our sanctuaries because acknowledging it might bring reproach on the church. And let us not succumb to the temptation to excuse violence under the cloak of cheap grace. Even though law enforcement, the judicial system, and our Christian communities fail to hear and respond to the cries of victims, God hears . . . and the Lord ultimately brings justice to the perpetrators, as well as to those who have closed their ears and eyes to the abuse.

He Is Self-Absorbed and Lacks Remorse

Cain's response to God's judgment was just as egocentric as his response to God's initial rejection of the offering. Instead of expressing regret or remorse for murdering his brother, Cain cried out for mercy in the midst of the consequences levied against him. He wasn't sorry for what he had done; he was only sorry that he had been caught and forced to accept the punishment. He never seemed to view himself as the guilty party; instead, he reacted as if he were the victim. Totally self-absorbed, Cain begged for God's protection—even though he himself had offered no such protection to Abel. That God was gracious enough to extend that protection speaks profoundly of the Lord's mercy, even while the abuser is yet an unrepentant sinner. Pastors and counselors, don't be drawn in by an abuser's efforts to portray himself as a victim, but also remember God's grace even to a remorseless man of violence.

He Refuses Advice

This is perhaps the most challenging characteristic of an abuser. Like Cain, who disregarded the counsel and caution of God himself, an abuser is all too often resistant to accepting advice or intervention. God was Cain's personal life coach and counselor, who urged Cain to deal with his anger lest it destroy him. The Lord warned Cain that evil was crouching at his door waiting to devour him. But God also showed Cain the way of escape—by taking charge of his anger and ruling it instead of allowing it to rule him. Cain had a choice—to *do* what was right or to follow his need to *be* right. If Cain could walk away from a powerful counseling session with God and commit fratricide, pastoral counselors should not be surprised if the abusers to whom they are ministering also walk away and continue in a life of violence. That is why agreeing to enter counseling is not a sufficient gesture of good faith; the victim's safety still is at risk. Just because an abuser agrees to talk with a counselor does not mean that he is hearing what is said or intending to change his behavior based on the counsel received. The abuser, like Cain, becomes his own god and trusts in his own heart. He may claim to believe in God, but he still needs to submit his whole heart, soul, mind, and strength to the Lord and allow God to transform his thinking. He needs spiritual direction from a godly pastor or counselor who points him to Jesus as the ultimate role model for how to be a good husband and father. He must also dig into the Scriptures to explore the character of God and the servant leadership style of Jesus. He must use the Word as a guide for his personal holiness instead of as a weapon of condemnation against his wife.

As you, pastor or counselor, look beyond the symptoms of a victim or abuser to the spiritual battle waged in that person's soul, ask God for wisdom and pray for discernment. Examine your motives for entering the counseling relationship. Are you interested in coming up with the right answer, fixing the problem, or looking good—or is your priority to lead the wounded person into an encounter with God? Before your first counseling session, make it your first priority to know God yourself and pray that your service will flow out of your passion for him.

Getting involved in the spiritual struggle of the victim or abuser is messy, risky, and time-consuming. Is it worth it? Jesus thought so when he gave up the glory of heaven to rescue the broken and the lost. He has released the power of his resurrection within us and uses our inadequacies to display his strength. For his glory, we can walk alongside others who need help and hope on the journey. For all Christ has done for us, how can we do less?

Note

1. "Spiritual Direction," in *Train the Trainer: FOCUS Support Group Leaders' Training Manual* (Elmhurst, IL: FOCUS Ministries, Inc., 2004), 97.

CHAPTER 12

What Does the Bible Say?

Instead of looking the other way and pretending the problem doesn't exist, or deliberately ignoring the problem to keep the family together at all costs, we need to search the living Word to find out what Jesus would do.

—*FOCUS Newsletter,* August/September 1998

Throughout this book you have read our words, quotations from writers, pastors, and musicians, and the stories of real people who have suffered from family violence so that you can understand more about how to effectively minister to families in crisis.

While they may convey our best thoughts and opinions, our words have no power to change lives. The only source containing words of truth and life is the Bible, and the only one who can change the heart and mind of a person is God. So let's dig in and see what God thinks about violence and oppression.[1] As you read, ask God to reveal himself to you through Scripture, especially in the example set by Jesus' life as portrayed in the Gospels.

Violence

The psalmist declares, "The LORD tests the righteous, but his soul hates the wicked and the one who loves violence" (Psalm 11:5). Of course, we are all sinners and wicked in contrast to God's holiness. The wicked person described here seems to be someone who pursues violence in the same way that the righteous pursue justice and mercy. That is what the prophet was talking about when he declared, "Violence has grown up into a rod of wickedness" (Ezekiel 7:11).

No wonder Ezekiel later carries the message from God, "Thus says the Lord GOD: Enough, O princes of Israel! Put away violence and oppression, and execute justice and righteousness. . . ." (Ezekiel 45:9). This is a divine call to those who love violence—to put away that desire to act out with tight fists or harsh words. God calls the rulers of the land, the princes themselves, to exchange violence and oppression for justice and righteousness. That is how God wants us to govern, and that is how God expects us to relate to one another—in the church, in the world, and in our own homes.

Lest there be any doubt on that point, look at Paul's job description for the church leader: "Therefore an overseer must be above reproach, the husband of one wife, sober-minded, self-controlled, respectable, hospitable, able to teach, not a drunkard, not violent but gentle, not quarrelsome, not a lover of money" (1 Timothy 3:2-3). "Not violent but gentle," Paul said clearly. Leaders, whether they are pastors, spouses, or parents, should be in control of their tempers, not looking for an argument or fight, welcoming and generous to others, and able to teach—by word and example—how to be a servant leader in the family of God.

Oppression

God is always on the side of the oppressed. There are more than two thousand verses in the Bible dealing with the oppressed and poor. Look again at Ezekiel 45:9: "Thus says the Lord GOD: Enough, O princes of Israel! Put away violence and oppression, and execute justice and righteousness. . . ." Notice the connection that God makes between violence and oppression. Anyone who has been a victim of verbal, emotional, psychological, or financial abuse understands the destructive power of oppression. It may not be evident in physical bruises or open cuts to show the world—but often the wounds of oppression are much deeper and slower to heal.

The psalmist assures us that God "has pity on the weak and the needy, and saves the lives of the needy. From oppression and violence he redeems their life, and precious is their blood in his sight" (Psalm 72:13-14). In another psalm, we have the promise, "The LORD works righteousness and justice for all who are oppressed" (Psalm 103:6).

What about the oppressor? What can that person expect from God? The prophet Isaiah brings this word from the Lord: "When you spread out your hands, I will hide my eyes from you; even though you make many prayers, I will not listen; your hands are full of blood. Wash yourselves; make yourselves clean; remove the evil of your deeds from before my eyes; cease to do evil, learn to do good; seek justice, correct oppression; bring justice to the fatherless, plead the widow's cause" (Isaiah 1:15-17).

"Cease to do evil, learn to do good; seek justice, correct oppression," the prophet urges. And that word not only summons the abuser to repentance, but it also calls the church to action—to follow the example of Jesus himself who included in his job description, "to set at liberty those who are oppressed" (Luke 4:18). That is one reason the Spirit of God rests on us—to minister healing and freedom to those who have been pressed down.

Verbal Abuse

God takes verbal abuse seriously; we should do the same. Scripture often links abusive language to the condition of the heart. In Matthew 15:18-20, Jesus taught, "But what comes out of the mouth proceeds from the heart, and this defiles a person. For out of the heart come evil thoughts, murder, adultery, sexual immorality, theft, false witness, slander. These are what defile a person. But to eat with unwashed hands does not defile anyone."

Solomon contrasts the mouth of the righteous and wicked person in Proverbs 10:11: "The mouth of the righteous is a fountain of life, but the mouth of the wicked conceals violence." The psalmist describes verbal abuse as a form of oppression in Psalm 10:7: "His mouth is filled with cursing and deceit and oppression; under his tongue are mischief and iniquity." Verbal abuse was a serious issue in the early church, prompting James to write a stern rebuke in his letter to fellow believers: "If anyone thinks he is religious and does not bridle his tongue but deceives his heart, this person's religion is worthless" (James 1:26).

Because verbal abuse is so crazy making (as James 3:10 says, "from the same mouth come blessing and cursing"), counselors should consider it as brutal as physical battering and more damaging to a woman's mental health.

Anger

One of the more obvious traits of an abuser is uncontrolled anger or rage, which is made more dangerous when embedded in a foolish heart. Scripture makes this point clearly in Proverbs 29:11: "A fool gives full vent to his spirit, but a wise man quietly holds it back."

The person who is filled with anger or rage in unable to reflect the righteousness of God. "Know this, my beloved brothers: let every person be quick to hear, slow to speak, slow to anger; for the anger of man does not produce the righteousness that God requires" (James 1:19-20). Thus, pastoral counselors would be wise to echo the wisdom of Solomon to both abuser and victim alike. To the perpetrator, you might urge, "Be not quick in your spirit to become angry, for anger lodges in the bosom of fools" (Ecclesiastes 7:9). To the potential victim or other men in your congregation, offer the warning: "Make no friendship with a man given to anger, nor go with a wrathful man, lest you learn his ways and entangle yourself in a snare" (Proverbs 22:24-25).

Victims

Encourage victims of abuse to see themselves as God's temple, which should never be desecrated. "Do you not know that you are God's temple and that God's Spirit dwells in you? If anyone destroys God's temple, God will destroy him. For God's temple is holy, and you are that temple" (1 Corinthians 3:16-17).

Victims might find empathic comfort from the cry of the psalmist who described the horror of being assaulted by a loved one:

My heart is in anguish within me; the terrors of death have
    fallen upon me.
Fear and trembling come upon me, and horror
    overwhelms me.
And I say, 'Oh, that I had wings like a dove!
I would fly away and be at rest; yes, I would wander
    far away;
I would lodge in the wilderness;
I would hurry to find a shelter from the raging wind
    and tempest.' . . .
For it is not an enemy who taunts me—then I could bear it;
it is not an adversary who deals insolently with me—
    then I could hide from him.
But it is you, a man, my equal, my companion,
    my familiar friend.

—Psalm 54:4-8, 12-13

Abusers

It is important for counselors to recognize the traits of an abuser in
order to see beyond an often charming exterior. The psalmist
describes such a person in this way: "Therefore pride is their neck-
lace; violence covers them as a garment. . . . They scoff and speak
with malice; loftily they threaten oppression" (Psalm 73:6-8).
Proverbs depicts the abuser as "quarreling" (20:3) and "wise in his
own eyes." These verses name many of the common characteristics
of an abusive person: prideful, violent, arrogant, foolish, verbally
abusive, threatening, oppressive, quarrelsome, and self-righteous.

The New Testament offers another profile of a self-absorbed
person with an abusive mindset:

> For people will be lovers of self, lovers of money, proud, arrogant,
> abusive, disobedient to their parents, ungrateful, unholy, heartless,
> unappeasable, slanderous, without self-control, brutal, not loving
> good, treacherous, reckless, swollen with conceit, lovers of pleas-
> ure rather than lovers of God, having the appearance of godliness,
> but denying its power. Avoid such people. (2 Timothy 3:2-5)

This passage not only exposes the heart of an abuser but also clearly warns us to "avoid such people." Why? Scripture describes the effects of intimacy with an abuser in Proverbs 13:20: "Whoever walks with the wise becomes wise, but the companion of fools will suffer harm."

Psalm 55:20-21 describes the experience of relationship violence in bitter words: "My companion stretched out his hand against his friends; he violated his covenant. His speech was smooth as butter, yet war was in his heart; his words were softer than oil, yet they were drawn swords." An abuser may appear kind and charming in public, but behind closed doors, he continuously violates the marriage covenant with treachery and various forms of violence.

Justice

When the human spirit is crushed by violence and oppression, victims cry out to God for help. How does God respond? "O LORD, you hear the desire of the afflicted; you will strengthen their heart; you will incline your ear to do justice to the fatherless and the oppressed, so that man who is of the earth may strike terror no more" (Psalm 10:17-18).

God responds with justice for the oppressed, strength for the brokenhearted, and a listening ear to the afflicted. Why? Because justice is a part of God's very character: "Righteousness and justice are the foundation of your throne; steadfast love and faithfulness go before you" (Psalm 89:14). Isaiah reiterates this assurance when he declares, "But the LORD of hosts is exalted in justice, and the Holy God shows himself holy in righteousness" (5:16).

The psalmist cried out to God on behalf of the oppressed, "May he defend the cause of the poor of the people, give deliverance to the children of the needy, and crush the oppressor!" (Psalm 72:4). As God's people, we must embrace this plea as our own mandate: "Give justice to the weak and the fatherless; maintain the right of the afflicted and the destitute. Rescue the weak and the needy; deliver them from the hand of the wicked" (Psalm 82:3-4).

As reassuring as it is to know that God's justice will ultimately prevail, as the body of Christ on earth, the church is responsible for being God's hands and feet in responding to the cries of the broken and hurting. "To do righteousness and justice is more acceptable to the LORD than sacrifice" (Proverbs 21:3).

When we fail to respond, God is displeased—and we can expect to be held accountable.

"Justice is turned back, and righteousness stands afar off; . . . The LORD saw it, and it displeased him that there was no justice. He saw that there was no man, and wondered that there was no one to intercede. . ." (Isaiah 59:14, 16). As the body of Christ, God expects us to take action and get involved in the lives of hurting people.

> If you take away the yoke from your midst, the pointing of the finger, and speaking wickedness, if you pour yourself out for the hungry and satisfy the desire of the afflicted, then shall your light rise in the darkness and your gloom be as the noonday. And the LORD will guide you continually and satisfy your desire in scorched places and make your bones strong; and you shall be like a watered garden, like a spring of water whose waters do not fail. And your ancient ruins shall be rebuilt; you shall raise up the foundations of many generations; you shall be called the repairer of the breech, the restorer of streets to dwell in. (Isaiah 58:9-12)

Sermon Ideas

- **Genesis 4:** Cain—the first violent man. An excellent sermon called "The Challenge of Raising Cain" by Pastor Erwin Lutzer of Moody Church is available online at http://moody-church.org in the audiotape series *Suffering Wrong*.
- **Isaiah 59:1-15:** Describes verbal violence (vv. 3-4) and God's hatred of violence (vv. 1-2).
- **Isaiah 59:15-21:** God's call for justice in response to violence.
- **Psalm 56:** God can be relied upon to defend the oppressed.
- **Isaiah 58:** God calls his people to action in responding to the needs around them.
- **1 Samuel 25:** Abigail is a good role model to show how a godly woman takes responsibility for her own actions, takes

a stand against evil, and does what is right with a gracious attitude. Her bravery saved her whole household from the foolish decisions of her abusive husband.

- **Proverbs:** Do a word study in the book of Proverbs on the words *fool, foolish,* or other derivatives of *fool.* One of the best books on this topic is called *Foolproofing Your Life* by Jan Silvious.[2]
- **Malachi 2:13-16:** Many sermons on God's view of divorce are based on this text. Make sure the last half of verse 16 is included in your sermon. Yes, God does hate divorce, but he also hates violence and treachery. Who is the witness between a treacherous man and his wife? God himself!
- **Ephesians 5:** Dig a little deeper in this passage and expound on the characteristics of Jesus as he interacts with his bride, the church. List specific ways a man should behave toward his wife, and list behaviors and attitudes that are inappropriate. Be very clear that all abuse is wrong and is never justified by another person's behavior.

Caution to Pastors

When you preach a sermon about the role of men and women in the home, be aware your words may be misinterpreted by an abusive man who believes you are upholding his right to rule his home and have dominion over his wife. After reading Scriptures such as Ephesians 5:22-33, Colossians 3:18-19, and 1 Peter 3:1-7, be sure to clearly define what it means for men to love their wives as Christ loved the church. Give examples of what constitutes abusive behavior and contrast that with the behavior of a servant leader, using Jesus as your example. Unless you are specific about ways a man should *not* treat his wife, the abuser will focus on his wife's failings and lose sight of his own.

When dealing with the subject of submission, be aware that the abuser believes his wife is his property and feels he is entitled to punish her for not agreeing with his opinions or fulfilling his demands. He may feel it is his God-given right to keep his wife in line, even if it involves violence. Yet nowhere in the Scriptures does

God allow men to punish their wives for lack of "submission" or for any other reason. Be clear in your preaching and teaching to emphasize how Jesus loved the church—not by laying down the law or raising his fists but by laying down his life and rising again on the third day.

Study the life of Jesus as he related to the disciples and others with whom he came in contact. He was direct and spoke truth with compassion and kindness. Even though the disciples spoke and acted foolishly at times, Jesus did not treat them with contempt or verbally abuse them. He was a servant leader who washed his disciples' feet instead of demanding special attention for himself. Jesus showed great respect to women and gave them a place of honor and service instead of giving them a subordinate role in the kingdom.

As you study the character of God and the example of Jesus, may you strive to imitate Christ in your own life and teach it diligently to men and women, boys and girls, in your congregation.

Notes

1. Scripture quotations in this chapter are from The Holy Bible, English Standard Version, copyright © 2001 by Crossway Bibles, a division of Good News Publishers. Used by permission. All rights reserved.
2. Jan Silvious, *Foolproofing Your Life: Wisdom for Untangling Your Most Difficult Relationships* (Colorado Springs: Waterbrook Press, 1998).

Preventing Family Violence

The devastation of family violence is too great to pretend it doesn't exist. The price of ignorance . . . is too high to remain uninvolved!

—*FOCUS Newsletter,* March 2002

As we witness the trauma of human suffering, our question is not "Where is God?" but "Where are God's people?" If our hearts are broken as we minister to families whose lives have been shattered, how much more deeply must God's heart ache?

What has God stirred in your heart as you have read this book? What will be your response? Are you willing to give up some comfort of your own to make a difference in the life of another?

The needs of families in crisis due to domestic violence will always be greater than the resources we have, but we can do *something.* Each of us can start with what we have . . . a listening ear, a spare bedroom, extra food in your pantry, funds to help with rent or lodging, transportation to an appointment, compassion that reflects Jesus' love in action.

But let us not be content with just meeting needs as they arise. We must take proactive steps to teach our children and young people how to have healthy relationships based on God's design and through our example. We must take a bold stand in our pulpits against violence and disrespect. We must clearly define the role of men and women in the home as they mutually reflect Jesus' model of submission and servant leadership. We must uphold justice for the oppressed and extend mercy to the broken. We must create a place of safety in our churches where both victims and perpetrators can seek help and find hope.

We are committed to the ministry of hope that God has set before us. Will you join with us? Together we can make a difference.

If you take away the yoke from your midst,
    the *pointing of the finger,* and *speaking wickedness,*
if you pour yourself out for the hungry
    and satisfy the desire of the afflicted,
then shall your light rise in the darkness
    and your gloom be as the noonday.
And the LORD will guide you continually
    and satisfy your desire in scorched places
    and make your bones strong;
and you shall be like a watered garden,
    like a spring of water,
    whose waters do not fail.
And your ancient ruins shall be rebuilt;
    you shall raise up the foundations of many generations;
you shall be called the *repairer of the breech,*
    the *restorer of streets* to dwell in.

—Isaiah 58:9-12 (ESV, italics added)

Resources to Help Victims

* Crisis Flow Chart

* Personal Safety Plan for Women and Children

* Needs Assessment Checklist

* The Effects of Domestic Violence on Children

* Red Flags for Parents and Teens

* Domestic Violence Organizations and Ministries

Crisis Flow Chart

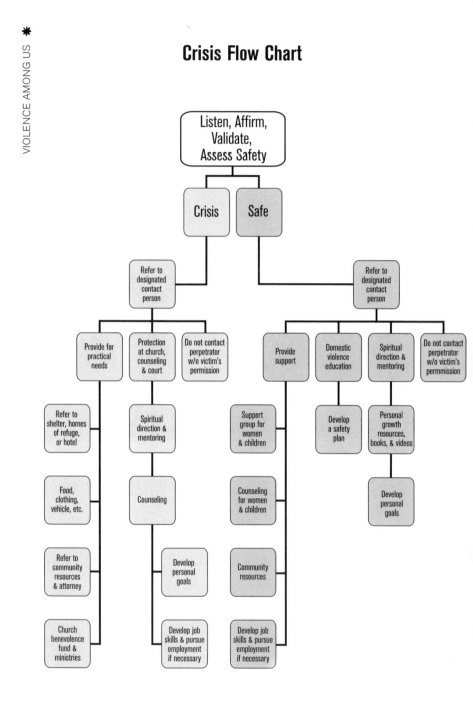

Personal Safety Plan for Women and Children

An expanded, eight-page safety plan is available as a free download at http://focusministries1.org.

1. If I decide to leave, I will get out of the house by _____
   _____.

2. I will keep my purse and car keys _____
   so I can get to them quickly when I have to leave.

3. I will tell _____ about the violence
   and ask them to call the police if they hear anything
   suspicious coming from my house.

4. I will use _____ as a code word for my children
   or friends to call 911 immediately.

5. If I have to leave my home, I will go to _____
   _____.

6. If I cannot go there, I will go to _____
   _____.

7. When an argument begins, I will go to _____
   _____, a room where I can safely exit.

8. I will leave money, an extra set of car and house keys, a
   change of clothing, and important papers with _____
   _____.

9. I will open a savings account by _____
   and begin saving something each month.

10. _____ will let me stay with them on an emergency basis.

11. I can leave extra clothes with _____
_____.

12. I will tell _____ at school,
_____ at church,
_____ at the
daycare center which people have permission to pick up
my children.

13. I will inform _____ (friend),
_____ (neighbors), and
_____(pastor) if my
husband no longer lives with me.

14. I will inform _____ (at work)
whether to accept calls or answer personal questions
from my husband and whether to allow him to visit my
workplace.

15. The phone number for the closest shelter is
_____.

16. Other phone numbers are
_____ (pastor),
_____ (supervisor),
_____ (friend),
_____(other).

Things-to-Take Checklist

☐ Identification for yourself and the children

☐ Birth certificates

☐ Marriage certificate

☐ Social Security cards (yours and children's—write down spouse's number)

☐ School and health records

☐ Money (In community property states, you can legally take half of the funds in a joint checking and savings account.)

☐ Checkbook and ATM card

☐ Credit cards (those held jointly and separately)

☐ Copies of unpaid bills, receipts, credit card statements, etc.

☐ Keys to car, house, lock box, storage building, etc.

☐ Registration and title to your car(s)

☐ License plate number on, and information about, spouse's car

☐ Medication

☐ Passport, will, recent photographs of spouse

☐ Medical records

☐ Deed to house and other real estate

☐ Mortgage papers

☐ Loan agreements

☐ Bank books (joint and personal accounts, children's accounts)

☐ Insurance policies

☐ Address book

☐ Pictures, videotapes, CDs, music, sentimental mementos

☐ Children's favorite toys and blankets

☐ Tax returns for the past three years

☐ Cancelled checks and bank statements for past five years

☐ Pay stubs (yours and his)

☐ Journals or diary

☐ Documentation of criminal activity, copies of police reports

☐ Copies of financial documents and portfolios; credit union accounts; 401(k) plan, profit-sharing, and pension information

Needs Assessment Checklist

Pastors, counselors, and others can use this form to determine the immediate needs of victims of domestic violence and how to meet them.

Needs	Yes	No	Comments

Safe Location:
   Women's shelter
   Private home			

Temporary Housing:
   Apartment
   Spare room			

Transportation:
   Car
   Driver			

Clothing			
Food			
Counselor			
Attorney			
Employment			
Money to pay bills			
Support Group			

Repairs:
   Car
   Household			

Safe, supportive person:
   Family
   Friend			

The Effects of Domestic Violence on Children

Effects of Domestic Violence on Younger Children

0–1 Year Olds

Ways of Being Drawn In	Effects of Abuse
• Seeing it	• Physical injury
• Hearing it	• Death
• Being awakened by it	• Fright
• Being injured by it	• Being traumatized by it
• Being ripped from mother's arms	• Sleep disturbances
• Having toys broken	• Eating disturbances
• Being born prematurely	• Being colicky or sick
• Being hit while in mom's arms	• Insecurity because of being cared for by a
• Being thrown	traumatized mom

2–4 Year Olds

Ways of Being Drawn In	Effects of Abuse
• Seeing it	• Acting out violently
• Hearing it	• Withdrawal
• Trying to stop altercation	• Trouble with other kids
• Becoming abused themselves	• Delayed toileting
• Being used as a physical weapon agaisnt the victim	• Eating problems
	• Nervous, jumpy
• Being interrogated by perpetrator about victim's activities	• Sleep problems
	• Insecurity, fear, and depression

5–12 Year Olds (continued page 124)

Ways of Being Drawn In	Effects of Abuse
• Seeing and hearing it	• Fear and insecurity
• Picking 1 parent to defend	• Low self-esteem
• Physically intervening	• Withdrawal/depression
• Calling the police	• Running away
• Running to neighbors for help	• Early drug/alcohol use

Reprinted from Family Refuge Center, www.familyrefugecenter.com.
Used by permission.

5–12 Year Olds (continued)

Ways of Being Drawn In	Effects of Abuse
• Being used as a spy against mom • Forced to participate in attack on mom • Being physically or sexually abused to control mom • Being restricted from contact with others	• School problems • Bed-wetting • Sexual activity • Becoming caretaker of adults

Effects of Domestic Violence on Older Children

Teens (Boys and Girls)

Ways of Being Drawn In	Effects of Abuse
• Killing/trying to kill perpetrator • Trying to stop the abuse • Hitting parent or siblings • Becoming physically abused • Being used as a spy • Being used as a confidant • Being coerced by perpetrator to be abusive to mom	• School problems • Social problems • Sexual activity • Shame and embarrassment • Truancy • Superachiever at school • Tendency to get into serious relationships too early to escape home • Depression • Suicide • Alcohol/drug use • Confusion about gender roles
Effects Specific to Boys Only	**Effects Specific to Girls Only**
• Learning that males are violent • Learning to disrespect women • Using violence in his own relationships • Confusion or insecurity about being a man • Attacking parents or siblings	• Learning that male violence is normal • Learning that women don't get respect • Accepting violence in her own relationships • Embarrassed about being female • Becoming pregnant

Red Flags for Parents and Teens

"It was past closing time, so not many people were around. And he was angry. I could see it in his eyes. He sat me down and gave it to me straight. It was then I saw the real him . . . he hit me, head butted me twice and got in my face, screaming bitter words of hatred. I have never been so scared. He grabbed me by the shoulders and slammed me into a nearby wall. Then he closed his hands around my throat and began banging my head against the wall. My eyes were watering. I couldn't breathe. I thought I was going to die."

These are not the words of a woman who has been abused by her husband—rather these are the haunting words of a teenager describing a violent incident that took place in the high-school hallway and involved her boyfriend.

To help teens trapped in the clutches of dating violence, parents need to be on the alert for danger signs. To avoid unhealthy relationships, teens need to learn how to recognize the red flags of abusive behavior.

Watch the Signs!

Parents, is your daughter involved in an abusive relationship?

- Does she seem afraid of her boyfriend at times?
- Does he make most of the decisions about what they will do and where they will go?
- Does he call frequently and demand to know where she is?
- Does she give up activities that were once very important to her (sports, music, etc.)?
- Does she spend all her time with her boyfriend and very little time with girlfriends?
- Have you heard her explaining every detail of her day to her boyfriend and trying to make him understand why she was later than she expected in getting home?
- Does she make excuses for his behavior (anger, jealousy, etc.)?

- Have you seen or heard him losing his temper toward your daughter or someone else?
- Has her appearance changed? Does she need his approval for the clothing and makeup she wears?
- Does she have unexplained injuries or bruises?
- Does she seem depressed or anxious?
- Does she criticize herself?
- Does she refuse to talk about the relationship?

Girls, does your boyfriend . . .

- Punch, kick, grab, choke, or exert physical control over you?
- Degrade you in private but turn on the charm in public?
- Insult your beliefs or friends?
- Ridicule women in general?
- Constantly ignore your feelings but expect you to always be considerate of his?
- Threaten to hurt you if you don't do what he says? Threaten your family or friends?
- Prevent you from leaving his presence or block the doorway so you can't get through?
- Threaten you with a weapon?
- Use drugs or alcohol?
- Control where you go, whom you talk to, and what you do?
- Enjoy pornography?
- Keep track of your time and the money you spend?
- Expect you to look and act a certain way?
- Become overly jealous and possessive?
- Restrict you from extracurricular activities (sports, music) or outings with your friends unless he is along?

- Constantly accuse you of cheating on him, flirting with other guys, dressing provocatively?
- Have frequent mood swings (switching from being calm to rage-filled in a moment's notice)?
- Blame his problems on other people?
- Have a parent who is abusive in the home?
- Enjoy hurting or killing animals for no reason?
- Become easily irritated—small things set him off?
- Need to control all the decisions and circumstances?

Surveys show that at least 28 percent of teen relationships involve violence (at least one in every four). What a tragic legacy we have passed on to the next generation!

Domestic Violence Organizations and Ministries

Faith-Based Organizations

Awake, Inc., Alpharetta, GA
http://www.awakeonline.org

Bridging the Gap Ministries, Tyler, TX
http://bridgingthegap.freeservers.com

Deborah's Place, Chicago, IL
http://www.deborahsplace.org

FaithTrust Institute, Seattle, WA
http://www.faithtrustinstitute.org

Family Renewal Shelter, Tacoma, WA
http://www.domesticviolencehelp.org

FOCUS Ministries, Inc., Elmhurst, IL
http://www.focusministries1.org

Foundation for Hope, Laguna Niguel, CA (Hope's House)
http://www.foundationforhope.com

Hosea's House, Louisville, KY
http://hoseashouse.org

Institute on Domestic Violence in the African American
    Community, St. Paul, MN
http://www.dvinstitute.org

Jewish Women International, Washington, DC
http://jwi.org

PASCH (Peace and Safety in the Christian Home), Brewster, MA
http://peaceandsafety.com

Safe Haven Ministries, Grand Rapids, MI
www.safehavenministries.org

Safe Place Ministries, Boise, ID
http://www.safeplaceministries.com

The Black Church and Domestic Violence Institute, Atlanta, GA
http://www.bcdvi.org

Time to Fly Foundation, Washington, DC
http://www.timetofly.org

Under His Wings Ministries, Indianapolis, IN
E-mail: rita@minister.com OR rlbowman@usa.com

WellSpring Center for Hope, Chicago, IL
http://www.wellspringcenterforhope.org

Women's Faith Force Ministry, Nashville, TN
http://womensfaithforceministry.org

Secular Organizations

Children

The Hideout (for children of abuse)
http://www.thehideout.org.uk/

National Committee to Prevent Child Abuse
Tennyson Center for Children at Colorado Christian Home
http://www.childabuse.org

National Youth Violence Prevention Resource Center,
   Rockville, MD
http://www.safeyouth.org

Prevent Child Abuse America, Chicago, IL
http://www.preventchildabuse.org

Red Flag Green Flag Resources, Fargo, ND
http://www.redflaggreenflag.com

Adults

American Bar Association Commission on Domestic Violence
http://www.abanet.org/domviol/victims.html

Family Violence Prevention Fund, Boston, MA;
   San Francisco, CA; Washington, DC
http://www.endabuse.org

National Coalition Against Domestic Violence
http://www.ncadv.org

National Domestic Violence Hotline
http://www.ndvh.org

National Network to End Domestic Violence, Washington, DC
http://www.nnedv.org

State Coalition List

The Alabama Coalition Against Domestic Violence
Hotline: (800) 650-6522
Website: www.acadv.org

Alaska Network on Domestic Violence and Sexual Assault
Website: www.andvsa.org

Arizona Coalition Against Domestic Violence
National toll-free: (800) 782-6400
Website: www.azcadv.org

Arkansas Coalition Against Domestic Violence
National toll-free: (800) 269-4668
Website: www.domesticpeace.com

California Partnership to End Domestic Violence
National toll-free: (800) 524-4765
Website: www.cpedv.org

Colorado Coalition Against Domestic Violence
In-state toll-free: (888) 788-7091
Website: www.ccadv.org

Connecticut Coalition Against Domestic Violence
In-state hotline: (888) 774-2900
Website: www.ctcadv.org

Delaware Coalition Against Domestic Violence
In-state toll-free: (800) 701-0456
Website: www.dcadv.org

DC Coalition Against Domestic Violence
Website: www.dccadv.org

Florida Coalition Against Domestic Violence
In-state toll-free: (800) 500-1119
Website: www.fcadv.org

Georgia Coalition Against Domestic Violence
Hotline: (800) 334-2836
Website: www.gcadv.org

Hawaii State Coalition Against Domestic Violence
Website: www.hscadv.org

Idaho Coalition Against Sexual and Domestic Violence
National toll-free: (888) 293-6118
Website: www.idvsa.org

Illinois Coalition Against Domestic Violence
Mayor's Office on Domestic Violence
In-state hotline: (877) 863-6338
Website: www.ilcadv.org

Indiana Coalition Against Domestic Violence
In-state toll-free: (800) 332-7385
Website: www.violenceresource.org

Iowa Coalition Against Domestic Violence
In-state hotline: (800) 942-0333
Website: www.icadv.org

Kansas Coalition Against Sexual and Domestic Violence
Website: www.kcsdv.org

Kentucky Domestic Violence Association
Website: www.kdva.org

Louisiana Coalition Against Domestic Violence
In-state toll-free: (888) 411-1333
Website: www.lcadv.org

Maine Coalition to End Domestic Violence
In-state toll-free: (888) 834-4367
Website: www.mcedv.org

Maryland Network Against Domestic Violence
National toll-free: (800) 634-3577
Website: www.mnadv.org

Jane Doe Inc.
The Massachusetts Coalition Against Sexual Assault and
Domestic Violence
Website: www.janedoe.org

Michigan Coalition Against Domestic and Sexual Violence
Website: www.mcadsv.org

Minnesota Coalition for Battered Women
National toll-free: (800) 289-6177
Website: www.mcbw.org

Mississippi Coalition Against Domestic Violence
In-state toll-free: (800) 898-3234; Monday-Friday,
    8 a.m. to 5 p.m.
In-state toll-free: (800) 799-7233, after hours
Website: www.mcadv.org

The Missouri Coalition Against Domestic and Sexual Violence
Website: www.mocadv.org

Montana Coalition Against Domestic and Sexual Violence
National toll-free: (888) 404-7794
Website: www.mcadsv.com

Nebraska Domestic Violence Sexual Assault Coalition
(402) 476-6256
Website: www.ndvsac.org

Nevada Network Against Domestic Violence
In-state toll-free: (800) 500-1556
Website: www.nnadv.org

New Hampshire Coalition Against Domestic
    and Sexual Violence
In-state toll-free: (866) 644-3574
Website: www.nhcadsv.org

New Jersey Coalition for Battered Women
In-state toll-free: (800) 572-7233
Website: www.njcbw.org

New Mexico Coalition Against Domestic Violence
Website: www.nmcadv.org

New York State Coalition Against Domestic Violence
In-state toll-free: (800) 942-6906 English
In-state toll-free: (800) 942-6908 Spanish
Website: www.nyscadv.org

North Carolina Coalition Against Domestic Violence
National toll-free: (888) 232-9124
Website: www.nccadv.org

North Dakota Council on Abused Women's Services
National toll-free: (888) 255-6240
Website: www.ndcaws.org

Action Ohio Coalition for Battered Women
In-state toll-free: (888) 622-9315
Website: www.actionohio.org

Ohio Domestic Violence Network
In-state toll-free: (800) 934-9840
Website: www.odvn.org

Oklahoma Coalition Against Domestic Violence
and Sexual Assault
Website: www.ocadvsa.org

Oregon Coalition Against Domestic and Sexual Violence
In-state hotline: (888) 235-5333
Website: www.ocadsv.com

Pennsylvania Coalition Against Domestic Violence
National toll-free: (800) 932-4632
In-state toll-free: (800) 537-2238
Website: www.pcadv.org

Rhode Island Coalition Against Domestic Violence
In-state toll-free: (800) 494-8100
Website: www.ricadv.org

South Carolina Coalition Against Domestic Violence
and Sexual Assault
National toll-free: (800) 260-9293
Website: www.sccadvasa.org

South Dakota Coalition Against Domestic Violence
& Sexual Assault
National toll-free: (800) 572-9196
Website: www.southdakotacoalition.org

Tennessee Coalition Against Domestic and Sexual Violence
In-state toll-free: (800) 289-9018
Website: www.tcadsv.org

Texas Council on Family Violence
In-state toll-free: (800) 525-1978
Website: www.tcfv.org

Utah Domestic Violence Council
In-state toll-free: (800) 897-5465
Website: www.udvac.org

Vermont Network Against Domestic and Sexual Violence
Hotline, domestic: (800) 228-7395
Hotline, sexual: (800) 489-7273
Website: www.vtnetwork.org

Virginia Sexual and Domestic Violence Action Alliance
National toll-free: (800) 838-8238
Website: www.vadv.org

Washington State Coalition Against Domestic Violence
In-state hotline: (800) 562-6025
Website: www.wscadv.org

West Virginia Coalition Against Domestic Violence
Website: www.wvcadv.org

Wisconsin Coalition Against Domestic Violence
Website: www.wcadv.org

Women's Coalition of St. Croix (U.S. Virgin Islands)
Website: www.wcstx.com

Wyoming Coalition Against Domestic Violence
  and Sexual Assault
National toll-free: (800) 990-3877
Website: www.wyomingdvsa.org

Resources to Help Perpetrators

* Characteristics of an Abuser

* Signs He Has Changed

* Batterer Treatment Programs and Ministries

Characteristics of an Abuser

He has a *negative attitude toward women* in general. He may believe women are inferior to men and mention this idea in the form of jokes.

He frequently *criticizes or humiliates* her for her opinions or actions that displease him.

He *says negative things* about her friends and family.

He *makes fun* of her ideas and dreams for the future.

He is *jealous* of her time and attention.

He is *very possessive* and tells her what she can and can't do. He may demand they do everything together.

He can fly into an *angry rage* unexpectedly for no apparent reason.

He *threatens* her with physical abuse and uses verbal abuse constantly.

He believes God has given him the *right to discipline h*er when she gets "out of line."

He may have destroyed her personal property or killed her favorite pet as a form of *punishment.*

He may be very *charming, easygoing, and overly affectionate* in public but turns into a *controlling tyrant* at home.

He may have *punched holes* in the walls at home and *broken things* by throwing them across the room.

He may have a *problem with alcohol or drugs* that intensifies his violent behavior.

He *blames* other people (especially his wife) for all his problems.

He is likely to have grown up in a *family where abuse was experienced or witnessed.*

He *minimizes or denies* his own abusive actions.

He feels *entitled* to get what he wants, especially from his family.

Signs He Has Changed

He is willing to wait however long it takes for her trust in him to be rebuilt and does not pressure her to forgive or reconcile until she is ready.

He does not say or do things that threaten or frighten her.

He listens to and respects her opinion, even if he disagrees.

She can express anger or frustration toward him without being punished or abused.

He respects her "no" in all situations, including physical contact.

He does not prevent her from spending time with friends and family and does not punish her later.

He is willing to continue counseling as long as necessary.

He takes responsibility for his actions and does not blame her for his bad behavior.

He is kind and attentive instead of being demanding and controlling.

When he becomes frustrated or angry, he does not take it out on his wife or children.

When he fails, he admits his mistake and takes responsibility for changing his behavior.

He admits to his abusive behavior and stops trying to blame others or to cover it up.

He acknowledges that all the abuse was wrong and identifies all the ways he used to justify his abusive behavior.

He acknowledges that his abusive behavior was not a loss of control but a choice on his part.

He recognizes and is able to verbalize the effects of his abuse on his spouse and children.

He identifies attitudes of entitlement or superiority and talks about the tactics he used in maintaining control.

He replaces distorted thinking with a more positive and empathetic view.

He consistently displays respectful behavior toward his wife and children.

He wants to make amends for the harm he has caused.

He is committed to not repeating his past behavior and realizes it will be a lifelong process.

He is willing to hear feedback and criticism, is honest about his failures, and is willing to be held accountable for abusive thinking and behavior.

Batterer Treatment Programs and Ministries

Guidelines for Choosing a Program

- The victim will be warned if threats of violence are made against her.

- The batterer signs a contract before beginning the program that he will commit to (1) perfect attendance, (2) refraining from abuse of alcohol and drugs, (3) nonviolence, and (4) signing a waiver of confidentiality on issues involving the safety of his victim.

- Treatment is in a group setting with a male-female team or two male facilitators.

- Couples counseling is not done, but facilitators interview victims separately to gather information about patterns of abuse.

- Curriculum focuses on power and control issues instead of anger management.

- Consequences for noncompliance are clearly stated and enforced.

- Successful completion includes being violence free for a set amount of time.

- The program is a minimum of 24 to 26 weeks with an additional period of follow-up where individual counseling is available if necessary.

Faith-Based Treatment Programs

Dr. Tommy Snow
Genesis 8 LLC
487 Winn Way, Suite 101
Decatur, GA 30030

Awake, Inc.
http://www.awakeonline.org

Secular Agencies

Emerge
2464 Massachusetts Ave., Suite 101
Cambridge, MA 02140
(617) 547-9879

Domestic Abuse Intervention Project
(known as the Duluth Model)
202 East Superior St.
Duluth, MN 55802
(218) 722-2781
http://www.duluth-model.org

Texas Council on Family Violence
P.O. Box 161810
Austin, TX 78716
(512) 794-1133
http://www.tcfv.org

Media Resources

* Books

* Audiotapes, Videotapes, and DVDs

* Training Manuals

* Seminars and Retreats

Books

Adams, Carol J. *Woman Battering*. Minneapolis: Fortress Press, 1994.

Alsdurf, James and Phyllis Alsdurf. *Battered Into Submission: The Tragedy of Wife Abuse in the Christian Home*. Downers Grove, IL: InterVarsity Press, 1989.

Bancroft, Lundy. *Why Does He Do That? Inside the Minds of Angry and Controlling Men*. New York: G. P. Putnam's Sons, 2002.

———. *When Dad Hurts Mom: Helping Your Children Heal the Wounds of Witnessing Abuse*. New York: G. P. Putnam's Sons, 2004.

Betancourt, Marian. *What to Do When Love Turns Violent: A Practical Resource for Women in Abusive Relationships*. New York: HarperPerennial, 1997.

Berry, Dawn Bradley. *The Domestic Violence Sourcebook*. Lincolnwood, IL: Lowell House, 2000.

Brewster, Susan. *To Be an Anchor in the Storm: A Guide for Families and Friends of Abused Women*. New York: Ballantine Books, 1997.

Canfield, Muriel. *Broken and Battered: A Way Out for the Abused Woman*. West Monroe, LA: Howard Publishing, 2000.

Clark, Ron. *Setting the Captives Free: A Christian Theology for Domestic Violence*. Eugene, OR: Cascade Books, 2005.

Cloud, Henry, and John Townsend. *Boundaries: When to Say Yes, When to Say NO to Take Control of Your Life*. Grand Rapids: Zondervan, 1992.

———. *Boundaries in Marriage*. Grand Rapids: Zondervan, 1999.

———. *Changes That Heal*. Grand Rapids: Zondervan, 1992.

———. *It's Not My Fault*. Nashville: Integrity Publishers, 2007.

———. *Safe People*. Grand Rapids: Zondervan, 1995.

Crabb, Larry. *Inside Out*. Colorado Springs: Nav Press, 1988.

———. *The Papa Prayer*. Brentwood, TN: Integrity Publishers, 2006.

———. *The Pressure's Off*. Colorado Springs: Waterbrook Press, 2002.

———. *Shattered Dreams*. Colorado Springs: Waterbrook Press, 2001.

———. *SoulTalk*. Brentwood, TN: Integrity Publishers, 2003.

Dutton, Donald G., and Susan K. Golant. *The Batterer: A Psychological Profile*. New York: HarperCollins, 1995.

Engel, Beverly. *The Emotionally Abused Woman: Overcoming Destructive Patterns and Reclaiming Yourself*. New York: Fawcett Columbine Book, 1990.

———. *The Emotionally Abusive Relationship: How to Stop Being Abused and How to Stop Abusing*. Hoboken, NJ: John Wiley & Sons, 2002.

Evans, Patricia. *The Verbally Abusive Relationship: How to Recognize It and How to Respond*. Holbrook, MA: Adams Media Corporation, 1996.

Fortune, Marie M. *Keeping the Faith: Guidance for Christian Women Facing Abuse*. New York: HarperSanFrancisco, 1987.

Gaddis, Patricia Riddle. *Battered but Not Broken: Help for Abused Wives and Their Church Families*. Valley Forge, PA: Judson Press, 1996.

———. *Dangerous Dating: Helping Young Women Say No to Dangerous Dating*, Colorado Springs: Shaw, 1984.

Grady, Jay. *Stop Verbal Abuse: How to Break the Cycle of Verbal Abuse*. Houston: Therapeia Publishing, 2003.

Hegstrom, Paul. *Angry Men and the Women Who Love Them: Breaking the Cycle of Physical and Emotional Abuse*. Kansas City, MO: Beacon Hill Press, 1999.

Jacobson, Neil and John Gottman. *When Men Batter Women: New Insights into Ending Abusive Relationships*. Simon & Schuster, 1998.

Kaufman, Carol Goodman. *Sins of Omission: The Jewish Community's Reaction to Domestic Violence*. Boulder, CO: Westview Press, 2003.

Klassen, Heather. *I Don't Want to Go to Justin's House Anymore*. Washington, DC: Child and Family Press, 1999.

Kroeger, Catherine Clark, and Nancy Nason-Clark. *No Place for Abuse: Biblical and Practical Resources to Counteract Domestic Violence*. Downers Grove, IL: InterVarsity Press, 2001.

Levy, Barrie, and Patricia Occhiuzzo Giggans. *What Parents Need to Know about Dating Violence: Advice and Support for Helping Your Teen*. Seattle: Seal Press, 1995.

McDill, S. R., and Linda McDill. *Dangerous Marriage: Breaking the Cycle of Domestic Violence*. Grand Rapids: Fleming H. Revell, 1991.

Miller, Mary Susan. *No Visible Wounds: Identifying Nonphysical Abuse of Women by Their Men*. New York: Fawcett Columbine, 1995.

Rinck, Margaret J. *Christian Men Who Hate Women*. Grand Rapids: Zondervan, 1990.

Scott, Sandra. *Charmers and Con Artists and Their Flip Side*. Enumclaw, WA: Winepress Publishing, 2000.

Silvious, Jan. *Foolproofing Your Life: Wisdom for Untangling Your Most Difficult Relationships*. Colorado Springs: Waterbrook Press, 1998.

Statman, Jan Berliner. *The Battered Woman's Survival Guide: Breaking the Cycle*. Dallas: Taylor Publishing Company, 1995.

Stewart, Donald. *Refuge: A Pathway Out of Domestic Violence & Abuse*. Birmingham: New Hope Publishers, 2004.

Townsend, John. *Who's Pushing Your Buttons?* Nashville: Integrity Publishers, 2004.

Vernick, Leslie. *The Emotionally Destructive Relationship: Seeing It, Stopping It, Surviving It*. Eugene, OR: Harvest House, 2007.

Weitzman, Susan. *"Not to People Like Us": Hidden Abuse in Upscale Marriages*. New York: Basic Books, 2000.

Audiotapes, Videotapes, and DVDs

General

Boundaries, www.cloudtownsendstore.com. Faith-based; request "old" version, which was taped before a live audience (unlike the new version produced by Zondervan).

Fool-Proofing Your Life, www.JanSilvious.com. Faith-based.

Safe People, www.cloudtownsendstore.com. Faith-based.

Victims

Bridging the River of Silence, www.kineticvideo.com.

Broken Vows: Religious Perspectives on Domestic Violence, www.faithtrustinstitute.org.

Defending Our Lives, www.cambridgedocumentaryfilms.org/defending.html.

Domestic Violence: What Churches Can Do, www.faithtrustinstitute.org.

In and Out of Control: Emotional, Physical, and Sexual Violence, www.kineticvideo.com.

Intimate Partner Violence (Dr Is In), www.kineticvideo.com.

It's Not Like I Hit Her!, www.kineticvideo.com.

Survival from Domestic Violence: Stories of Hope and Healing, www.kineticvideo.com.

Survivors: Women Overcoming Domestic Abuse, www.kineticvideo.com.

Turning Point: Women Who Abuse, www.kineticvideo.com.

Violence Against Women, www.kineticvideo.com.

Wings Like a Dove: Healing for the Abused Christian Woman, www.faithtrustinstitute.org.

Perpetrators

Room Full of Men, www.kineticvideo.com.

Time to Change, www.kineticvideo.com.

Turning Point: Women Who Abuse, www.kineticvideo.com.

Waking Up to Violence, www.kineticvideo.com.

Teens

Teens Speak Out: Dating Violence,
   http://www.breakthecycle.org/curriculum_video.html.
Violence in the Family, www.kineticvideo.com.
When Push Comes to Shove, www.jwi.org. Faith-based. Look
   under the Toolkit Curriculum section of the website.

Children

Eternal Scars: Physical and Emotional Child Abuse,
   www.kineticvideo.com.
I Wish the Hitting Would Stop, www.redflaggreenflag.com.
Impact of Violence on Children, www.kineticvideo.com.
It's Not Okay: Let's Talk About Domestic Violence,
   www.abanet.org.
What About Us? www.kineticvideo.com.

Training Manuals

From FOCUS Ministries, Inc. (www.focusministries1.org)

Pastor's Guide—Dealing with Domestic Violence
   (available in English and Polish)
Support Group Leader's Guide
FOCUS Resource Manual
Manual on Domestic Violence

From Awake (www.awakeonline.org)

Shepherd's Case Planner
Men's Case Planner
Women's Case Planner

From the National Coalition Against Domestic Violence (www.ncadv.org)

Teen Dating Resource

Seminars and Retreats

From FOCUS Ministries, Inc. (www.focusministries1.org)

A Woman's Journey to God

Domestic Violence Task Force Consultation
(look under Pastor's Toolbox)

Domestic Violence Training for Pastors and Churches
(look under Pastor's Toolbox)

Train the Trainer. For FOCUS Support Group Leaders

Women's conferences and retreats. Topics vary.

From Other Organizations

End Needless Oppression, Unite God's House Conferences
(www.awakeonline.org)

Domestic Violence Seminars and Training
(www.peaceandsafety.com)

Domestic Violence and Child Abuse Seminars and Training
(www.faithtrustinstitute.org)

Domestic Violence Training (www.pollysplacenetwork.com)

Domestic Violence Training (www.safeplaceministries.com)